SALMAN RUSHDIE

SALMAN RUSHDIE

Damian Grant

© Copyright 1999 by Damian Grant

First published in 1999 by Northcote House Publishers Ltd, Horndon, Tavistock, Devon, PL19 9NQ, United Kingdom.
Tel: +44 (0) 1822 810066 Fax: +44 (0) 1822 810034.

Reprinted 2007

British Library Cataloguing-in-Publication Data
A catalogue record for this book is available from the British Library

ISBN 978-0-7463-0797-7

Typeset by PDQ Typesetting, Newcastle-under-Lyme
Printed and bound in the United Kingdom

For Fiona, Fergus, and Marcus

Contents

Acknowledgements

I am grateful to the University of Manchester for the grant of sabbatical leave during 1997. Also to the universities of Burgundy and Lille, York, and again Manchester, for invitations to conferences at which some of the material included here was proposed and discussed. I would also like to express my thanks for the conversation and encouragement of Madeleine Descargues. She knows what we both owe to Sterne and Rushdie; resembling Padma in nothing else, she has talked this project forwards.

Biographical Outline

1947   Salman Rushdie born in Bombay, the only son of Anis Ahmed Rushdie, a businessman who had received his education in Cambridge, and his wife, Negin. There are three sisters in the family.

1954   Rushdie attends an English Mission school in Bombay.

1961   Rushdie sent to England for his secondary education, at Rugby School.

1964   The family moves to Pakistan: Karachi.

1965   Goes to Cambridge (King's College) to read history. No longer a believer, develops a historical interest in Islam. Becomes involved in acting with the Cambridge Footlights, and addicted to the cinema.

1968   Returns to Pakistan; works briefly in television before returning to London, where he joins a company of actors.

1969   Works as a copywriter for advertising agencies, taking time out to write a first (unpublished) novel on Indian themes.

1970   Meets Clarissa Luard.

1974   Five-month trip to India and Pakistan.

1975   February: first published novel *Grimus*. Political involvement with black and Asian groups in London.

1976   April: Marries Clarissa Luard.

1979   June: son Zafar born. Gives up copywriting job to write fiction full-time.

1981   February: *Midnight's Children* published to critical acclaim. October: wins the Booker Prize.

1983   September: third novel *Shame* published. Begins work on what was to become *The Satanic Verses*.

1984   Travels to Australia with the writer Bruce Chatwin. Meets Robyn Davidson.

1986   Travels to Nicaragua at the invitation of the Sandinista

Association of Cultural Workers. Meets the American novelist Marianne Wiggins.

1987   January: *The Jaguar Smile: A Nicaraguan Journey* published.

1988   Divorced from his first wife. Marries Marianne Wiggins. September: *The Satanic Verses* published. The novel is denounced in India and Pakistan, and burnt in the street in Bradford.

1989   14 February: announcement of the *fatwa* against Rushdie by the Ayatollah Homeini, and offer of a reward by the State of Iran for his murder. Rushdie goes into hiding, under the protection of the British Government with Special Branch police bodyguards. The 'Rushdie Affair' attracts international attention, stimulating anti-Islamic feeling in the west. Formation of Rushdie support groups in England, France, and elsewhere. The British Government makes representations to Iran without success. Separation from Marianne Wiggins.

1990   Publication of several books on the Rushdie Affair. September: *Haroun and the Sea of Stories* published.

1991   March: *Imaginary Homelands: Essays 1981–1991* published; includes a last section devoted to essays and addresses which provide Rushdie's own perspective on his situation.

1992   March: *The Wizard of Oz* published by the British Film Institute.

1994   October: collection of stories *East, West* published.

1995   September: *The Moor's Last Sigh* published.

1996   Writes introduction to *Burning Your Boats*, the collected short stories of his friend Angela Carter, who had died in 1992.

1997   Publication of anthology *The Vintage Book of Indian Writing 1947–97*, edited with Elizabeth West. Marries Elizabeth West. July: second son Milan born. September: writes controversial article in *The New Yorker* on the death of Princess Diana in a car accident, linking this event with David Cronenberg's film of J. G. Ballard's novel *Crash*.

1998   February: on the ninth anniversary of the *fatwa*, which is reasserted in Iran, Rushdie meets Tony Blair to discuss diplomatic moves. Speaking on BBC television, declares his belief in the absolute right of free speech. September: the Iranian Government officially distances itself from the *fatwa*. Rushdie says: 'It looks like it's over. It means everything. It means freedom.'

Abbreviations

EW   *East, West* (London: Jonathan Cape, 1994)

G.   *Grimus* (London: Paladin, 1989)

HSS   *Haroun and the Sea of Stories* (London: Granta Books/ Penguin, 1990)

IH   *Imaginary Homelands: Essays and Criticism 1981–1991* (London: Granta Books, 1991)

JS   *The Jaguar Smile: A Nicaraguan Journey* (London: Picador, 1987)

MC   *Midnight's Children* (London: Jonathan Cape, 1981)

MLS   *The Moor's Last Sigh* (London: Jonathan Cape, 1995)

S.   *Shame* (London: Picador, 1984)

SV   *The Satanic Verses* (London: Viking, 1988)

WO   *The Wizard of Oz* (London: BFI, 1992)

...some incredibly important things were being fought for here: being important to me, the art of the novel; beyond that, the freedom of the imagination, the great overwhelming, overarching issue of the freedom of speech and the right of human beings to walk down the streets of their own country without fear.

Salman Rushdie, *Guardian*, 26 September 1998

1

Introduction

Near the beginning of the nineteenth century, at a time not unlike our own of international tension and political uncertainty that entailed threats to personal liberty and freedom of thought, and when he himself had been victimized for atheism, the poet Shelley wrote a *Defence of Poetry*, which has become celebrated for its definition of the role of the imagination in the discovery and direction of our lives. Laws and conventions deriving from 'ethical science' may be necessary, he concedes, for the conduct of 'civil and domestic life', but it is the imagination that unlocks our full humanity. 'A man, to be greatly good, must imagine intensely and comprehensively', divining a more profound morality beyond the scope of rational requirement. 'The great instrument of moral good is the imagination; and poetry administers to the effect by acting upon the cause.'[1] And at the end of the twentieth century, many wars, revolutions, and anathemas later, we are if anything even more aware that the active exercise of the imagination is indispensable to the realization, establishment, and defence of those values which define us and according to which we try to live our lives. In what amounts to a near paraphrase of Shelley, the subject of this study, Salman Rushdie, insists that the imagination, 'the process by which we make pictures of the world ... is one of the keys to our humanity' (*IH* 143).

It is also true that the appeal to the imagination, then as now, invites rather than evades argument. In that extraordinarily modern document from the early eighteenth century, *A Tale of a Tub*, Swift identified the imagination as that which gives access to the whole spectrum of human potential, leading us 'into both extreams of High and Low, of Good and Evil'. As if to prove Swift's point, what Dr Johnson reproves as a 'licentious and vagrant faculty' is later enshrined as a principle of perception and expression by the romantics: Coleridge's 'shaping spirit of Imagination'.[2] But, from the start, apologists for the novel had invested less heavily in the imagination, relying more on observation and documentation – though Sterne's *Tristram Shandy*, with its focus on 'what passes in a man's own mind', provides an important qualifying instance. Emile Zola specifically ejected the imagination from his theory of the novel, arguing that a properly scientific method had no use for it.[3] In the present century, all the claims and counter-claims for and against the role of the imagination in fiction have become simultaneously available, from Henry James's sacramental views in *The Art of the Novel* (1934) through the liberties of the science-fiction writer, fantasist, or 'magic realist', to Samuel Beckett's paradoxical vision of the cessation of all mental activity in *Imagination Dead Imagine* (1965). And those writers sometimes described as 'from elsewhere', typically those with a post-colonial background, have a specially difficult negotiation to make in this respect. One thinks of the strenuous theorizing of the Guyanian writer Wilson Harris, who has argued that 'a philosophy of history may well lie buried in the arts of the imagination', and believes that the dynamism of cultural admixture 'lies in the evolutionary thrust it restores to the orders of the imagination'. Harris has both sponsored (in his essays) and exemplified (in his novels) that 'counter-culture of the imagination' which he sees as the most positive and creative response to the colonial experience, in what is to be understood as a 'quest for new values'.[4] And it is here, in this contested space, that we must locate the work of Salman Rushdie.

Rushdie's own formulations of his project most often involve reference to the imagination as the agent of synthesis or transformation. It is the imagination that liberates us from the crude 'facts' of history (other people's history), and that may even absolve us from the unredeemed diary of our own lives. It will be worthwhile, therefore, to consider what Rushdie has to say in his essays about the presiding power of the imagination, and then to see how this might help us in our approach to the novels. One of the things that we learn from these essays is that

2

for Rushdie, as a postmodern writer, there is no such thing as an unqualified fact, nor an absolute fiction; the two categories necessarily overlap and leak into each other. He quotes an apposite observation from Graham Greene in this respect: novelists and journalists are antagonistic, today, because 'novelists are trying to write the truth and journalists are trying to write fiction' (*IH* 217). Rushdie sees Julian Barnes's *History of the World in 10 ½ Chapters* as 'the novel as footnote to history', 'not a history but a fiction about what history might be' (*IH* 241). Calvino's Sister Theodora (in *The Non-Existent Knight*) writes her chivalric story from the protected ignorance of her convent, 'inventing the unknown, making it seem truer than the truth', while the Marquez whom Rushdie refers to as 'Angel Gabriel' has the ability, through the extraordinary power of his imagination, to 'make the real world behave in precisely the improbably hyperbolic fashion of a Marquez story' (*IH* 257, 300). Pynchon's novels represent for Rushdie 'a rich metaphorical framework in which two opposed groups of ideas [pessimistic entropy and optimistic paranoia] struggle for textual and global supremacy', and this novelist has the capacity to let these differently sponsored worlds inform each other; 'his awareness of genuinely suppressed histories ... always informed his treatment of even his most lunatic fictional conspiracies' (*IH* 269).

The novelist's mistrust of history is pervasive; but it is not only novelists who can challenge official versions of the truth. 'In the aftermath of the Kennedy assassination,' suggests Rushdie in the essay just quoted (on Eco), 'the notion that "visible" history was a fiction created by the powerful, and that ... "invisible" or subterranean histories contained the "real" truths of the age, had become fairly generally plausible'. But the novelist is the one explicitly dedicated to that form which 'allows the miraculous and the mundane to co-exist at the same level', in which 'notions of the sacred and the profane' can be simultaneously explored (*IH* 376, 417). And this is the basis of his own defence of *The Satanic Verses*:

> I genuinely believed that my overt use of fabulation would make it clear to any reader that I was not attempting to falsify history, but to allow fiction to take off from history ... the use of fiction was a way of creating the sort of distance from actuality that I felt would prevent offence from being taken. (*IH* 409)

3

Rushdie tersely adds here: 'I was wrong.' But whatever the risks involved in attempting a synthesis of fact and fiction, the separation of the two offers an even bleaker prospect. Facts by themselves will get the writer nowhere: 'where the strength for fiction fails the writer, what remains is autobiography.' The trouble with another writer's work, Rushdie protests, is that he 'will not let it take off ... he scarcely ever lets the fiction rip'; and 'the distrust of the narrative ... undermines all the intelligence, all the image-making, all the evocative anecdotes' (*IH* 150, 290). By the corresponding argument, fiction by itself – without the ballast of real history, the gravitas of real experience – will tend to float off into triviality. 'There is a difference between invention and imagination,' he maintains in another context; the first provides (even in a war reporter) 'make-believe', where the second will offer 'reliable accounts of the horrific, metamorphosed reality of our age' (*IH* 204). One thinks of the criticism of surrealism made by Wallace Stevens, that it 'invents without discovering'[5] – playing unserious games, conducting hypotheses with no control and therefore ultimately no interest.

It is the imagination that negotiates between the two categories, and Rushdie's cumulative account of the role and function of the imagination – in writers and film-makers alike – is almost always positive. The real frontiers of fiction 'are neither political nor linguistic but imaginative' (*IH* 69): the imagination knows how to transcend boundaries, in the way Wilson Harris argues it must if the new voices in the new literatures are to be heard in the world. It is only through an exercise of imagination that we can take part in the project of what is now a global culture, write the 'books that draw new and better maps of reality, and make new languages with which we can understand the world' (*IH* 100). The recurrent metaphor of the map reminds us just how territorial the imagination may be. In an important essay from 1985 entitled 'The Location of *Brazil*' (*IH* 118–25), on Terry Gilliam's futuristic film, Rushdie explains: 'It is not easy ... to be precise about the location of the world of the imagination. ... But if I believe (as I do) that the imagined world is, must be, connected to the observable one, then I should be able, should I not, to locate it; to say how you get from here to there.' The problem is, 'the more highly imagined a piece of work, the more ticklish the problem of location becomes'. Where is Oz, where is Wonderland? Where is *Apocalypse Now* set? Where, for that matter, should we locate Swift's Lilliput, or Samuel Butler's Erewhon: where are all those 'secondary worlds', as Tolkien called the fictional creations of the artist.[6] The spatial metaphor will obtain only so far; then there is a collision, a war between these worlds that will gravitate towards each other.

Gilliam's film tells us 'something very strange about the world of the imagination – that it is in fact *at war* with the "real" world, the world in which things inevitably get worse and in which centres cannot hold'. And this war is what literature is really about; whether in terms of the real wars of *War and Peace* and *The Red Badge of Courage* or the metaphorical wars of Milton and Blake: the war and peace in heaven and hell. Elsewhere, Rushdie quotes Richard Wright as saying that 'black and white Americans were engaged in a war over the nature of reality' (*IH* 13), and this is the war he sees himself as fighting in this essay. The compulsion of the artist tells him: '*Play. Invent the world.*' But the 'play' is serious: 'the power of the playful imagination ... to change forever our perception of how things are' has been demonstrated, he argues, by *Tristram Shandy* as well as by *Monty Python*. (It is an exemplary case that the novelist Sterne contended with the philosopher Locke precisely over the nature of the imagination, and the capacity of language to represent its processes.) For Rushdie, the modern world is 'as much the creation of Kafka ... as it is of Freud, Marx, or Einstein'. And it is at this point in his essay that Rushdie links the idea of change to that of the new 'migrant sensibility': 'the effect of mass migrations has been the creation of radically new types of human beings: people who root themselves in ideas rather than in places.' Virginia Woolf proposed that 'human character changed' in 1910;[7] Rushdie implies that 1947 would be a better date – or, the decade preceding this that saw such enforced migrations on a world scale. But this is, after all, a film review, and Rushdie concludes that the cinema itself is perhaps the place where the new may germinate: 'And for the plural, hybrid, metropolitan result of such imaginings, the cinema, in which peculiar fusions have always been legitimate ... may well be the ideal location.' If new sensibilities require new forms (as they do), then Rushdie is an enthusiastic proponent of these: not only film, but also radio, the gramophone, television, video ... all find their place as both narrative material, structural device, and metaphor in his fiction. And in the late twentieth century, this is indeed the location of culture. As Steven Connor remarks, if Rushdie exploits the media in his fiction it is because 'such forms are the evidence of a fundamentally new relationship between public and private life'.[8]

The argument of this essay lies at the heart of Rushdie's understanding and practice; as we shall see, all the significant critical disagreements can be referred back here, at least for clarification. It provides the argument to back his earlier assertion that 'Writers and politicians are natural rivals. Both groups try to make the world in their own images; they fight for the same territory' (*IH* 14). It also links Rushdie to the mainstream of post-colonial culture, where the spatial metaphor has a particular appositeness. Many writers within this tradition see the imagination as defining a 'space' which is more metaphorical than actual. Homi Bhabha quotes Wilson Harris on the need to face up to the 'void', the 'wilderness' of realities denied, in proposing his own idea of a 'Third Space', not hemmed in by simple dualities, where hybridity might truly thrive.[9] One might also compare the fertile idea of the 'Fifth Province of the Imagination' which has been proposed as the space in which to think our way beyond the categorical politics rooted in the four provinces of ancient Ireland.[10] Benedict Anderson's influential book *Imagined Communities* provides an elaborated model for how this imagination has been materialized in the very structure and self-identity of modern societies.[11] A good practical example of these tensions in action is provided by Rushdie's account of the ideological struggle in Nicaragua, which he observed on a visit in 1986 and wrote about in *The Jaguar Smile: A Nicaraguan Journey* (1987).

This is much more than just a travel book. While providing, certainly, a vivid descriptive account of the precarious situation in Nicaragua in June 1986, when the triumphant but beleaguered Sandinistas, in government under Daniel Ortez, were bracing themselves for the American invasion that never came, Rushdie's book is also a meditation on the process that goes into the making of a nation: and on how this process may (or may not) be compared to the 'making' of fiction. After the terror of the Somoza years, including the terror of 'nonentity' in the

Blakeian sense, when the country simply *'wasn't there'* (*JS* 157), the liberated people of Nicaragua 'were inventing their country, and, more than that, themselves'. 'At the Enrique Acuña co-operative...I had seen a people trying hard to construct for themselves a new identity, a new reality, a reality that external pressure might crush before construction work had even been completed' (*JS* 86, 96). The creative process reaches through all levels of society: agrarian, administrative, cultural, political; but, somehow, it is focused by the fact that so many of the politicians are also themselves artists: poets, novelists, painters, musicians. Rushdie is particularly struck by the proliferation of poets in Nicaragua, and even finds himself described at one point as *'hindú...poeta'* (*JS* 25). It may be appropriate to recall at this point another optimistic formulation from Shelley's *Defence of Poetry*: where he says that in 'the infancy of society every author is necessarily a poet...'.[12] It is almost as if the newly born Nicaragua is being created by its citizens as a work of art, like Morris's socialist Utopia or Yeats's mythical Byzantium. And, indeed, Rushdie does allow what Coleridge called the 'shaping spirit of Imagination' to direct his own discourse. 'It is impossible', he says after the 1972 earthquake and the Somoza ravages, 'not to see [the city of Managua] in symbolic terms'. Meanwhile the legendary Sandino, founder of the libertarian movement, has become 'a cluster of metaphors'; a priest delivers a homily which is 'an extended metaphor' of the political situation, made over in biblical and other parallels (*JS* 17, 22). Even the mountain range to the north of the country derives a 'mythic, archetypal force' from its association with the Sandinista rebels (*JS* 74). Five years on from *Midnight's Children*, Rushdie reminds us at the beginning of this book that 'I've always had a weakness for synchronicity' (*JS* 11), and it is not surprising that these aspects are foregrounded in the account that follows.

But (as in that novel) the patternless retributions of the real world are not to be avoided here. History is unlike fiction because (he quotes from C. V. Wedgwood) it 'is lived forward but it is written in retrospect'. And Nicaragua likewise has to face the future:

> The act of living a real life differed, I mused, from the act of making a fictional one, too, because you were stuck with your mistakes. No revisions, no second drafts. To visit Nicaragua was to be shown that

7

the world was not television, or history, or fiction. The world was real, and this was its actual, unmediated reality. *(JS* 168)

This is in stark contrast to the American perception of Nicaragua, as interpreted by an American film producer Rushdie meets: 'You've got to understand that for Americans, Nicaragua has no reality.... To them it's just another TV show. That's all it is.' This meeting takes place in the Somocista country club in Managua, where Rushdie also has a conversation with an elderly gentleman (he 'was, of course, a poet') who praises the Indian Writer Tagore – obstinately pronounced Tagoré – precisely for his realism. Rushdie responds: ' "Many people think of Latin America as the home of anti-realism," I said. He looked disgusted. "Fantasy?" he cried. "No, sir. You must not write fantasy. It is the worst thing. Take a tip from your great Tagoré. Realism, realism, that is the only thing." ' *(JS* 56) You must not write fantasy: realism is the only thing. The anonymous old man's advice faces Rushdie the novelist with his own bifurcating (or proliferating) options; and takes us back as readers to the critical alternatives in considering Rushdie's art.

And here, even if it is hidden away from the front line of conflict, there is still a war on. There are antagonists as well as allies engaged with equal passion over the disputed territory of the imagination, and everything that it represents, or comes to represent, in the real world. The most bitter and dangerous 'battle of the books' has been (and is still being) fought over *The Satanic Verses*. The ramifications and repercussions of the infamous *fatwa* are not the primary concern of this study, except in so far as this situation dramatizes issues that normally take a more muted form in criticism. Documents gathered in *The Rushdie File* (1989) remind us how central arguments over the imagination are to this debate. Ben Okri warns that 'we are in danger of passing a death sentence on the imagination'; and Carlos Fuentes underlines the double-edged importance accorded to 'the uses of the literary imagination': 'By making the imagination so dangerous that it deserves capital punishment, the sectarians have made people everywhere wonder what it is that literature can say that can be so powerful.'[13] And in *For Rushdie*, a parallel collection of articles by Arab, African, and French writers, Edward Said says simply: 'Rushdie is the *intifada* of the imagination', the focus of the imagination's holy war.[14] Although Rushdie has defended *The Satanic Verses* as a work of fiction, seeing the charges against the novel as a 'category mistake', he has also admitted that the novel has been caught up in 'an argument about who should have power over the grand narrative, the Story of Islam' (*IH* 432); and Sardar and Davies's combatively entitled *Distorted Imagination: Lessons from the Rushdie Affair* attacks Rushdie on precisely these grounds.[15] In what is one of the most deeply considered contributions to the debate, *A Brief History of Blasphemy*, Richard Webster reminds us that we need to exercise our own responsibility in these matters: 'We need to take back our imaginative powers from the artists, novelists and poets to whom we have delegated them. For there is a danger in delegating imaginative powers just as there is a danger in delegating any powers. We need our own imaginations.'[16]

Rushdie is, in fact, well aware of the double-edged quality of the powers which he exercises as an author, of what happens when 'we first construct pictures of the world and then...step inside the frames' (*IH* 378). But, while the process of argumentation is necessary, it is also true that it will never in itself resolve anything; and that, for a writer, in any case, 'the real risks...are taken in the work' (*IH* 15), in the complex and precarious navigation between real and fictional worlds. Rushdie has suggested that a book is a kind of passport, that gives us 'permission to travel' in the imagination (*IH* 276). Pursuing this metaphor, one might indeed suggest that Rushdie's novels are navigations not so much through space (though there are journeys and destinations) nor even through time (though this is their author's preferred dimension), but rather through levels of reality, dimensions in a more metaphysical sense – as perceived by the shifting sands of human consciousness.

This is not to say that the imagination itself is either innocent or infallible. As Rushdie said of *Midnight's Children*: 'I tried to make it as imaginatively true as I could, but imaginative truth is simultaneously honourable and suspect' (*IH* 10). In an excess of fervour or from the wrong kind of commitment, it may generate delusions as well as visions; and Rushdie is therefore prepared to stand in as prosecutor too. In the same essay where he proposes the imagination as the 'key to our humanity', he also concedes that 'the imagination can falsify, demean, ridicule, caricature and wound as effectively as it can clarify, intensify and unveil' (*IH* 143). He cites the notion of 'commonwealth literature' itself as an instance of imaginative perversity: the category is a 'chimera', a 'monstrous creature of the imagination...composed of elements which could not possibly be joined together in the real world' (*IH* 63). The British general election of 1983 was, in Rushdie's view, 'a dark fantasy, a fiction so outrageously improbable that any novelist would be ridiculed if he dreamed it up' (*IH* 159). The 1986 essay 'Debrett Goes to Hollywood' even betrays Rushdie's disenchantment, on this score, with the cinema. In the old days he says we allowed the stars to determine our reality for us: 'Banality made our lives unreal; *they* were the ones who were fully alive. So we munched our popcorn and grew confused about reality.' But the situation has now got out of hand: 'When murderers start becoming stars, you know something has gone badly wrong.... And when the techniques of starmaking, or image and illusion, become the staple of politics, you understand...' (*IH* 328); you understand, that is, that the imagination has been enlisted for corrupt or at best for futile purposes. Recalling the critique of media images made in Nicaragua, Rushdie quotes approvingly Michael Herr's castigation of the Vietnam represented on television and in film as a dangerous phenomenon. The media, says Herr, are guilty of deflecting the American public 'from any true meditation about what happened there', and so from any 'collective act of understanding'. The movies have provided a substitute experience for the war, but 'the war was not a movie. It was real' (*IH* 334–5). Even Saul Bellow is accused of 'investing his fiction with the absolute authority of reality', an instance of hubris in a writer; Naipaul likewise with purveying 'a novelist's truth masquerading as objective reality' (*IH* 351, 374). This represents perhaps a curious reversal of priorities; but it is also a useful reminder of the limitations which must be placed on the freedom of the imagination – which Rushdie is later prepared to theorize with reference to his own case. In the 1990 essay 'Is Nothing Sacred?' Rushdie asks himself whether his own instinctive belief in the 'absolute freedom of the imagination' might not represent a 'secular fundamentalism' with dangers of its own, 'as likely to lead to excesses, abuses and oppressions as the canons of religious faith' (*IH* 418). He comes back to argue that of all the art forms 'literature can still be the most free', and to assert that 'the interior space of the imagination is a theatre that can never be closed down' (*IH* 424, 426); but at the end of the essay he concedes that there is no privileged category: 'The only privilege literature deserves – and this privilege it requires in order to exist – is the privilege of being the arena of discourse, the place where the struggle of languages can be acted out.' (*IH* 427).

It is not only in the essays but in the novels themselves that Rushdie pursues the critique of the imagination – a theme we shall return to in the chapters that follow. Rushdie's first published novel *Grimus* is an exploration of the function of the imagination itself, an allegorical narrative of how the imagination can seek to detach itself from reality and create a 'world' of its own, outside time and accident, but immune also to the rhythm of creation in birth and death, and the love that embraces them. It is Rushdie's version of the familiar romantic myth of a space created by the imagination as a refuge from the responsibilities of the real world. This responsibility is fully assumed in *Midnight's Children*, where the imagination is enlisted to participate in the birth of a nation, macroscopically, and at the microscopic birth of one child (and his thousand magical siblings). The story of Saleem Sinai's first thirty years is synchronized with the first thirty years of independent India, with optimistic moments and dramatic reversals carefully cross-stitched in the narrative. But even here we are not to believe everything we are told. Saleem's father Ahmed Sinai is a victim of fantasy in his own life; his longing for 'fictional ancestors' leads him to 'invent a family pedigree that . . . would obliterate all traces of reality', and the narrator Saleem himself confesses at one point to telling self-protective lies: 'I fell victim to the temptation of every autobiographer . . . to create past events simply by saying they occurred' (*MC* 109–10, 427). The lesson to be drawn from this is that history is not only *made*, by events, but also *made up*, narrated, like the story of a life or the anecdotes within it. 'History is always ambiguous. Facts are hard to establish, and capable of being given many meanings. . . . The reading of Saleem's unreliable narration might be . . . a useful analogy for the way in which we all, every day, attempt to "read" the world' (*IH* 25). It is this creative combination that falls

11

apart in *Shame*. Pakistan, we are told, is a country that has been 'insufficiently imagined', and Rushdie's novel of near-Pakistan wrestles with a series of irreconcilable polarities: the two 'halves' of Pakistan itself, the deadlocked Harappa/Hyder families, and what Rushdie identifies as the competing male and female plots. Here, it may be suggested, there is no reconciling metaphor, no resolution back into history (where 'art dies back to life', in a phrase from a poem by D. J. Enright[17]); there is only the coruscation of shame itself, and the dubious promise of the novel's apocalyptic ending.

The operations of the mind itself, in its imaginative capacity, are brought into sharp focus again in *The Satanic Verses*, this time in a novel which is also densely realized in terms of both contemporary–historical and mythical–religious contexts. The imaginative threads and coherences that compose identity; the pivotal, polymorphous energies of the imagination producing both good and evil; the degrees of imaginative assent that constitute faith (and doubt) – all these interact in the novel, interrogating each other through different personalities (grouped around Gibreel Farishta and Saladin Chamcha), different locations (Bombay, London, 'Jahilia'), different historical periods, contrasted states of consciousness (waking/dreaming, sane/insane, ecstatic/suicidal). Caught at one moment in these currents, Gibreel exclaims 'if I was God, I'd cut the imagination right out of people' (*SV* 122): this is where all our dilemmas are identified. How to live our lives imaginatively but free of illusion? The novel elaborates on this theme in complex counterpoint and delivers what are in effect two endings, reflecting success or failure in this very negotiation. *Haroun and the Sea of Stories* provides a lighter but no less illuminating account of these proceedings. The imagination can be threatened by personal unhappiness and arbitrary power, but by the same token it possesses the resources to fight back against and overcome these tyrannies. And (to take a more optimistic view of the tension between generations), the comic dimension of this fairy tale for adults is endorsed by the fact that it is a son who frees his father on the troubled sea of stories, blessing the biological 'narrative' with the restoration of the gift of narrative itself. The stories in *East, West* provide their own versions of this imaginative enterprise, introducing us to multiple selves, alternative futures, instances of the problematic 'permeation of the real world by the fictional' (*EW* 94) which ask and hesitate to answer the familiar personal and cultural questions. In *The Moor's Last Sigh* Rushdie returns to the materials – and to some of the methods and motifs – of *Midnight's Children*, but with a very different imaginative as well as geographical perspective. There is once again a macro- and micro-narrative: this time, the greater history of the Spanish/Portuguese colonizing of Goa, and the smaller history of the Zogoiby family and firm, working the spice trade in Cochin. But what is different here is that Rushdie offers us a bifocal view of this twinned narrative, a developed metaphor for the imaginative assumption of experience. First there is the story itself, narrated in the first person by Moraes Zogoiby ('Moor'); then there is the visual record of some of these events, in the series of paintings made by his mother Aurora over many years, which are described in great detail in the text. These reflect both the history of modern India and her own anguished family story, offering at the same time a history and a critique of artistic representation itself – from the transformations of myth through social documentary and domestic drama to the imposition of a hard, ideological overlay. So that, when a character says 'I blame fiction' for the problems we bring on ourselves (*MLS* 351), we recall that the novels mean to engage us in a continuous discussion of the subject. And, although the imagination is the 'prime mover' in Rushdie's fiction, and in a sense always part of the subject itself, the novels contain their own critique of the fiction-making process, and a permanent reminder of our responsibility to the 'real world' – however this is to be recognized. As Steven Connor has remarked, 'At the heart of *Midnight's Children* is a curiously moralistic mistrust of the modes of the fabulous which it indulges with such zest'.[18]

Making our own navigation from the novels to a theory that might underpin them, we note that the arts of the imagination have to be identified and brought under discussion in formal terms – according to relevant conventions and expectations. One of the characters in *Grimus* expresses a preference for stories which are 'like life, slightly frayed at the edges, full of loose ends and lives juxtaposed by accident', over those stories which are 'neat', 'tight', and governed by 'some grand design' (*G.* 141). The alternatives set out here provide a useful grounding for the formal discussion of Rushdie's work – not least, because they expose what looks like a contradiction.

On the one hand, there is the familiar breaking down of formal categories, the endorsement of multiformity: the author proposes that the form of *Midnight's Children*, 'multitudinous, hinting at the infinite possibilities of the country', should be understood as 'the optimistic counterweight to Saleem's personal tragedy' (*IH* 16). Likewise, if Saleem's own vision is fragmentary, a 'broken mirror', nevertheless 'the broken mirror may actually be as valuable as the one which is supposedly unflawed' (*IH* 10). He suggests (in this same essay) that it is the mode of fantasy, 'or the mingling of fantasy and realism', that can best represent Indian reality, providing the necessary 'double perspective': 'this stereoscopic vision is perhaps what we can offer in the place of "whole sight"' (*IH* 19) – the 'whole sight' which is disowned as the delusive promise of omniscient Western realism. It is significant that Rushdie's defence of *The Satanic Verses* is also made primarily in formal rather than ideological terms. The novel – at least in the view of its author – 'celebrates hybridity, impurity, intermingling, the transformation that comes of new and unexpected combinations of human beings, cultures, ideas, politics, movies, songs'; it is (he says) 'a love-song to our mongrel selves' (*IH* 394). This becomes in a later essay ('Is Nothing Sacred?') a defence of the novel itself: 'the most freakish, hybrid and metamorphic of forms', which was 'created to discuss the fragmentation of truth', a form which realizes its true potential in 'challenging absolutes of all kinds' (*IH* 422–5). One is reminded of D. H. Lawrence, and the advocacy by another exiled and beleaguered writer of a form which he valued precisely for its being 'incapable of the absolute'.[19]

But our experience as readers of Rushdie's fiction insists that there is another principle at work within this centrifugal fragmentation. There is also a centripetal counter-movement which seeks to bring all these miscellaneous fragments into significant relation with each other. The obtrusive coincidences, synchronicities, the anticipations and recapitulations, all those elements which even the battered Saleem sees as part of the 'national desire for form', are the work of an organizing intelligence, and are as essential to the arts of the imagination as any other quality. Receptiveness and responsiveness, curiosity, have to be balanced, activated, by desire and design; as Coleridge reminds us, the imagination coordinates and subordinates as part of its task of invoking and celebrating.[20] Rushdie's own valuation of the 'centripetal' principle is clear not only from his own practice but also from comments made about other novelists. His debt to Sterne's *Tristram Shandy* is as significant as it is well documented,[21] because Sterne's objective in that novel is to mask order (art) with disorder (life), to be as he says 'digressive, and...progressive too, – and at the same time',[22] in effect reconciling two contrary principles. Rushdie's own version has it: 'to write in a form which appears to be formless' (*IH* 179). Rushdie has confessed to being 'very keen on the eighteenth century in general, not just in literature', and his comment on another eighteenth-century masterpiece, Fielding's *Tom Jones*, provides a useful sight into the writerly qualities he most admires:

> the thing that's very impressive about Tom Jones is the plot, you have this enormous edifice which seems to be so freewheeling, rambling – and actually everything is there for a purpose. It's the most extraordinary piece of organization which at the same time seems quite relaxed and not straitjacketed by its plot. I think that's why the book is so wonderful.[23]

Rushdie makes another instructive parallel between his own novelistic practice and that of Fielding and Sterne in a later interview when he observes, 'I spend much more time on the architecture of my books than on their writing. It takes me a very, very long time to understand the book...what connects with what and what the machine is. That's why it takes me five or six years to write one of those big books.'[24]

One has to conclude that the formal principles at work in Rushdie's fiction are more complex than might at first be supposed. Not only is there the endorsement of hybridity (the mixture of Western and Eastern forms, of written and oral modes; the mixture of 'fantasy and naturalism'; the mixture of genres and styles, of media and languages – all associating in an aleatory, linear time), but also the simultaneous appeal to order; to the structure of coincidence, to pattern, control; to the symmetry of biology, the purity of mathematical logic or geometric design – these having their fulfilment in the

15

complementary idea of time as cyclic and recurrent. This opposition, with its ethical and political as well as aesthetic coordinates, lies at the very heart of Rushdie's fiction, to be revolved in different ways in each of the novels. And it is also a theme that helps conduct the critical debate.

CRITICAL RESPONSES

Provocativeness is not without its perils, and it will surprise no one that the critical response to Rushdie's work includes all shades of opinion, delivered from a wide variety of viewpoints. Even if we set aside (as I shall do) the merely expletive attacks from those who have never actually read the work, there is still a body of informed opinion that takes objection to Rushdie's work on general, ideological grounds; and it might be useful to consider the nature of these objections before proceeding further. This will involve returning to Rushdie's claims for the imagination, which are contested by those who argue that the individual imagination is conditioned by other, underlying factors that need to be entered in the cultural equation before this faculty is allowed 'free play'. In what was the first important book on Rushdie, *Salman Rushdie and the Third World: Myths of the Nation* (1989), Timothy Brennan develops a critique of the kind of imaginative investment made (or not made) by Rushdie, Vargas Llosa, and other 'cosmopolitan writers of the Third World' whose attitude to the national myth exhibits what he calls a 'creative duplicity'.[25] With them, argues Brennan, the familiar figures of 'allusion, metaphor, allegorical parable are all like nationalism itself, "janus-faced"', with one face looking west. He quotes Gabriel Marquez's definition of the imagination against both Marquez himself and Rushdie: if Marquez believes that 'the imagination is nothing more than an instrument for elaborating reality', then it should be used more responsibly. 'Their shockingly inappropriate juxtaposition of humorous matter-of-factness and appallingly accurate violence, both ironically alludes to the blasé reporting of contemporary news and the preventable horrors of current events.'[26] Rushdie's *Midnight's Children* may, he says, have put 'the Indo-English imagination on the map', but only through being parasitic on earlier developments. Writing of

16

the Pakistan we meet in *Shame*, Brennan accuses Rushdie of destroying 'any coherence his imagination may have given the country by adopting a formal attitude that makes every statement capable of being at the same time withdrawn',[27] a revealing criticism (picking up the 'janus' image) which disallows – or simply fails to understand – the *inherent* duplicity of the imagination, as defined by Swift, developed by Sterne, and inherited by Rushdie from this and other traditions of story-telling. As Milan Kundera has argued, in fiction 'the unique truth is powerless', since the 'satanic ambiguity' which is the novel's privilege 'turns every certainty into enigma'.[28] It is significant that Brennan also objects to Rushdie's irony, endorsing Gramsci's preference for 'impassioned sarcasm' as 'the appropriate stylistic element for historical-political action'.[29] Aijaz Ahmad certainly seems to have schooled himself on sarcasm for his follow-up attack on Rushdie in *In Theory* (1992). The chapter on *Shame* in this book is a systematic attempt to disqualify Rushdie's writing through a closely argued but nevertheless tendentious analysis of his imaginative formation. 'How very enchanting', he reflects, 'Rushdie's kind of imagination must be' for readers brought up on a certain kind of modernist universalism. 'One did not have to belong, one could simply float, effortlessly, through a supermarket of packaged and commodified cultures, ready to be consumed'.[30] Ahmad challenges what he calls the 'grid of predispositions' which have gone into the making of such an imagination', on the way to rejecting 'the whole imaginative topography of modernism'.[31] Ahmad's own 'predispositions' are clearly otherwise, as is revealed in this summary of the situation in the attending novel, *Shame*:

> For so wedded is Rushdie's imagination to imageries of wholesale degradation and unrelieved social wreckage, so little is he able to conceive of a real possibility of regenerative projects on the part of those who actually exist within our contemporary social reality, that even when he attempts, towards the end of the novel, to open up a regenerative possibility, in the form of Sufiya's flight... the powers which he, as author, bestows upon her in the moment of her triumph are powers only of destruction.

Ahmad too is wrongfooted by Rushdie's ambivalence, protesting at the 'linguistic quicksand' in this novel, 'as if the truth of each utterance were conditioned by the existence of its opposite'[32] – a valuable insight, were it not offered ironically. (As Oscar Wilde reminded us, 'a Truth in art is that whose contradictory is also true'.)[33]

The work of Brennan and Ahmad may be taken as sufficiently representative of the denigration of Rushdie's work by certain 'post-colonial' critics – those who would tie in the novel form deterministically to Western ideological formations, and read individual novels for signs of their authors' ignorance, fallibility, or opportunism. Brennan challenges not only the critical reception but the very authenticity of writers such as Rushdie, Vargas Llosa, Carlos Fuentes, and Isabelle Allende, and what he reads as their implicit claim to 'represent' Third World realities. Drawing on Gramsci's analysis of the unaffiliated intellectual in Italy in the 1930s, who becomes 'cosmopolitan' because of the political fragmentation of that country, and also the adoption of the term by Frantz Fanon to describe the parasitic middle class in emergent African states, Brennan develops his own notion of the 'Third World cosmopolitan' as someone (whether politician, writer, or global industrialist) whose cultural allegiance is to a First World order, severed from any national, collective, or democratic reference. As a result, these values will tend to appear only in parodic or otherwise distorted forms. Rushdie has been selected by this critic as an example of a cultural and political argument of his own, and his criticism is heavily conditioned by a set of beliefs which perceive literature as 'politicized in the prescriptive sense', and functioning as 'a social institution with interventionary powers'.[34] Ahmad meanwhile blames Rushdie's descent from modernism for his 'bleak vision', his 'aesthetic of despair'. The 'highly pressuring perspective of modernism', he suggests, 'uses the condition of exile as the basic metaphor for modernity and even for the human condition itself', preventing any real engagement with history. Reading *Shame*, he objects, 'one is in danger of forgetting that Bhutto and Zia were in reality no buffoons, but highly capable and calculating men whose cruelties were entirely methodical'.[35] This puts one in mind of the blank objections raised against storytelling by Mr Sengupta in *Haroun and the Sea of Stories*: 'What's the use of stories that aren't even true?' (*HSS* 20). Mr Sengupta would have been ill-advised to become a literary critic. Taking up a similar post-colonial perspective in an essay called 'From Politics to Poetics', Tim Parnell likewise criticizes the way Rushdie's novels operate on the 'boundaries between the fictional and the historical'. For him, the novels' complexity reflects the 'labyrinth cunningly constructed by an imperial past', and thereby 'does appear to deny the peoples of India and Pakistan the possibility of escaping' from it. Somehow it becomes the fault of fiction that, for all its imaginative exploration, 'the established structures of power remain undisturbed'. And so Parnell concludes that the 'waning of Saleem's magic powers' in *Midnight's Children* 'might be read as a metaphor for the political limitations of Rushdie's attempts to harness postmodern poetics to a postcolonial political agenda'.[36]

It is worth recalling at this point James Harrison's very reasonable question: 'upon what compulsion ... must Rushdie meet the criteria for salvation specified by some post-colonial catechism?'[37] One is surely entitled to suspect criticism that fails to see what is actually there in a writer's work, and compounds that failure by lamenting the absence of something derived from its own prescription. Keith Wilson is a more reliable guide when he suggests that 'what Rushdie presumes in his reader, and what he makes the base of his narrative strategy, is an ability to read a text as literature, with an instinctive understanding of the nature of the process that is under way'.[38] It is only when we can read literature disinterestedly, with an awareness of this process, that we can safely negotiate between it and other discourses. Malise Ruthven provides the model for such a negotiation in the chapter 'Satanic Fictions' in his *A Satanic Affair* (1990). Ruthven begins from the position that, though Rushdie, while being a novelist, is also both journalist and activist, his fictional critique 'contains an ambivalence' that sets it apart, makes it something qualitatively different from the social intervention. It is the nature of novelistic discourse that 'form rather than content becomes the vehicle of dissent'.[39] He quotes a review by Brad Leithauser from the *New Yorker*, which argued that *The Satanic Verses* 'is so dense a layering of dreams and hallucinations that any attempt to extract an unalloyed line of argument is false to is intention'. He also cites Gayatri Spivak's view that there is 'no clear boundary between religion and fiction as products of the imagination' in the novel, on the way to arguing on his own account that the novel should be seen as 'a kind of "anti-

Qur'an" which challenges the original by substituting for the latter's absolutist certainties a theology of doubt.'[40]

And this takes us into the formal heart of the ideological argument. 'For the novel as a genre has an ideology – it is an ideology – of its own, one that lives by attacking the tendency of ideology itself to abandon "the wisdom of uncertainty" in the pursuit of a totalizing system.' Thus Michael Gorra in *After Empire*.[41] And, although this implies potential conflict with a whole range of ideologies, it is inevitably the dramatic conflict with militant Islam that has occasioned most commentary. One may cite Milan Kundera again: 'theocracy goes to war against the Modern Era and targets its most representative creation: the novel'.[42] The fundamentalist response to what Brennan calls the 'provocation' to Islam is documented in *The Rushdie File*, and developed in the extensive literature on the 'Rushdie Affair'.[43] But, if one is trying to defend a space for fiction, not just in theory but in conflictual praxis, one must acknowledge the intervention of those Islamic scholars who have themselves spoken up in Rushdie's defence. First published in French (with many articles translated from Arabic) in 1993, the volume *For Rushdie: Essays by Arab and Muslim Writers in Defense of Free Speech* is an impressive collection of nearly a hundred articles written from what the editors refer to as 'the currently devastated city that is Islam today' towards that fictional place where 'the prophetic gesture has been opened up to the four winds of the imaginary'.[44] It is from a similar perspective that Sadik Al-Azm defends Rushdie against the 'archaism' of Islam, linking him to a long tradition of writers and film-makers (from Rabelais to Scorsese) whose work represents a necessary challenge to repressive authority both religious and secular.[45] And in the course of an excellent, clarifying article on the issues surrounding *The Satanic Verses*, which relocates these in the discourse of satire itself, Srinivas Aravamudan asks the pertinent question: must there not be 'a polytheistic blasphemy lurking under every resolute monotheism?' It is significant that Aravamudan cites the authorial duplicities of Swift here, and the model of the anarchic imagination we have already referred to, in *A Tale of a Tub*.[46] The satirist is never innocent; but we must ask ourselves, of what exactly is he guilty? It is strange – almost perverse, in this context – that Stephanie Newell should suggest in her article

'The Other God: Salman Rushdie's "New" Aesthetic', that Rushdie sets up in *The Satanic Verses* a text which is to be read as a dogmatic alternative to the Koran itself; that Rushdie's 'all-controlling creative Ego', functioning as 'arbiter of reality', imposes a 'quasi-theological new Truth' upon the reader. This essay, often cited, is a good example of how a perverse reading can turn the text against itself, making a 'prison' (the term is actually used in the argument) of what is offered as an imaginative adventure.[47]

A second ideological construction that we need to consider is that of gender politics. The subject of gender represents, as we know, one of the most sensitive critical issues of our time, and it has to be said that Rushdie's work has sustained a good deal of adverse response in this connection. The narrator of *Shame* tells us that the ambiguous hero Omar Khayyam 'developed pronounced misogynistic tendencies at an early age' (*S*. 40), and it has become almost a critical reflex to pass on the charge to Rushdie himself (relating this, often, to the Islamic culture which provided him with his own formative experience). Catherine Cundy, in her otherwise even-handed treatment of Rushdie, is consistently critical of this aspect of his work. His 'tendency to demonize female sexuality', his 'ambivalence if not outright confusion', are, she says, declared in *Grimus*, repeated in *Midnight's Children* (where she defends even Indira Gandhi against presentation 'in such relentlessly misogynist terms'), and confirmed in *Shame*, where the 'blend of confusion, frustration, and even outright hostility' to women is 'more evident...than anywhere else'.[48] Which does not, however, spare the later novels. Cundy rests her case with the proposition that the treatment of women in Rushdie's novels 'serves more as a revelation (albeit involuntary) of Rushdie's psychology' than it contributes to the fiction.[49] The shallower side of this argument is exemplified by Inderpal Grewal, who decides for herself that 'what Rushdie writes for' is 'the improvement in the lot of Pakistani women', and then accuses him of failing to deliver. It is characteristic of such criticism that she goes on to prescribe the novel Rushdie should have written: 'If Rushdie had drawn upon a history of struggle instead of a history of subjection, his novel could have provided a myth of struggle and liberation that would have helped present and future struggles'.[50] Anuradha

21

Dingwaney Needham, on the other hand, is prepared to look beyond the declared and dramatized positions of Rushdie and his characters to the field of discourse within which these occur: 'We do not ... find a unitary, monolithic identity in Rushdie; rather, his work reflects a conception of post-colonial identity that is fluid, multiple, shifting, and responsive to varied situations and varied audiences.' For her, Rushdie does not create an 'utopian or visionary space' for women; he seeks rather 'to *expose* the particular and horrifying conditions of their oppression'. Needham concludes her essay with an account of her experience as reader and teacher of Rushdie's fiction. This has revealed that 'Rushdie's construction of post-colonial identities ... is particularly enabling', and his two novels *Midnight's Children* and *Shame* 'have turned out to be wonderful texts with which to begin and end a course on "Third World" literature in English'.[51]

It should be easier to characterize the response to Rushdie's fiction from a formal point of view, if only by default, in that even the adverse ideological criticism concedes the formal originality of his work. And there is indeed a consensus that, if Rushdie has 'put the Indo-English imagination on the map', it is substantially due to his mastery of the eclectic modes of fiction. But the very fact of Rushdie's eclecticism has actually made it difficult for critics to interpret Rushdie's formal project. In the introduction to his substantial collection of essays *Reading Rushdie*, M. D. Fletcher sets up a battery of formal terms, hesitating in his attribution between different categories as well as forms and styles: the postmodern and the post-colonial, metafictional strategies of various kinds (including parody), oral tradition and magic realism, forms of satire, polyphony, metamorphosis, and the grotesque.[52] And the essays themselves do not provide a more coherent picture. *Grimus* defeats critical ingenuity, Ib Johansen proposing it is 'a strange blend of mythical or allegorical narrative, fantasy, science fiction, and Menippean satire', while Catherine Cundy settles here for the formula 'chaotic fantasy'.[53] Peter Brigg sees *Midnight's Children* as a 'mixture of comedy, grotesque, and intellectual puzzle',[54] while *The Satanic Verses* is variously described as comic burlesque, an intermingling of fabulism and surrealism, encyclopaedic, carnivalesque, an example of 'enantiomorphism' (that is, characterized by oppositional structure), a 'Wo/manichaean novel', a Manichaean allegory, the apotheosis of gossip ('an underrated medium'), an epiphanic tragedy, and the first postmodern Islamic novel.[55] For all the ingenuity sometimes displayed in these formal identifications, there is little critical insight or real orientation offered to the reader. The more illuminating descriptions are provided by those critics who are less concerned to label the novels (like Saleem's pickle jars) but remain alert to their distinctive flavours, however these may be communicated. Sometimes this will be by impressionistic comparison, as when Uma Parameswaran compares the structure of *Grimus* to a Rubik cube, or when Keith Wilson finds the technique of 'literary pointillism' in *Midnight's Children*; with Patricia Merivale's 'comic zeugmas' and 'grotesque shifts of perspective' in the same novel;[56] with those critics elsewhere who have noted Rushdie's characteristic use of repetition, recapitulation, and prolepsis, as well as the distinctive palinode;[57] and those who have drawn attention to his debt to the art of cinema.[58]

Academic criticism has found Rushdie's fiction fertile ground for the study of influences and intertextual reference – much of it interesting and informative within the limited terms accepted by such an exercise. Rushdie's declared debts to Cervantes, Sterne, Joyce, Grass, and Marquez have been extensively (if not exhaustively) explored. However, the less obvious but no less pervasive influence of other writers deserves further study. One thinks not only of Shakespeare, and the exemplary eighteenth-century writers (other than Sterne) – that is to say, Defoe, Swift, and Fielding; but also of Blake and Dickens; Kafka and Bulgakov; Yeats, Beckett, and Ted Hughes: from all of these Rushdie has derived perspectives that are deeply set at thematic and even structural levels, as well as traceable verbally in the work. There has so far been no specific or extended treatment of Rushdie's interplay with any of these authors, which would certainly add to our appreciation and understanding. Meanwhile, it is that criticism that has been able to relate Rushdie's work to its Eastern as well as its Western sources which has proved a useful corrective to the kinds of cultural appropriation occasionally described above. Uma Parameswaran's 1988 collection of her own essays, *The Perforated Sheet*, is one valuable contribution here; as are the two pieces on Rushdie in Sara

Suleri's *The Rhetoric of English India* (1992). Both these authors feature in Fletcher's collection, alongside others (Aravamudan, Bharucha, Sadik Al-Azm) who represent Indian and Arabic traditions. *The Novels of Salman Rushdie* (edited by G. R. Taneja and Rajinder Kuman Dhawan, New Delhi, 1992) contains two dozen essays by mainly Indian critics, reprinted from two issues of the *Commonwealth Review* in 1990. One should also draw attention to articles which have appeared since 1980 in journals such as *ARIEL, The Journal of Commonwealth Literature, The Journal of Indian Writing in English, Kunapipi, Wasafiri, World Literature Today,* and *World Literature Written in English.*

LANGUAGE

All these critical explorations have to do in some measure with the recognition of Salman Rushdie's originality as a writer, whether this is defined in formal terms or according to Ashis Nandy's deep-field formula – the 'reinterpretation of tradition to create new traditions'.[59] But we cannot consider the nature of Rushdie's originality without finally making some reference to language itself, the writer's immediate and conditioning medium. The question proposed in *The Satanic Verses* – 'How does newness enter the world?' – presents itself first of all in linguistic terms. From *Grimus* onwards, Rushdie was in the business of inventing not just worlds but languages; the languages of groups, trades, professions, cliques, as well as the distinctive Dickensian idiolects of individuals. And language also makes itself available as metaphor for the creative process, when the midnight child is in the womb: 'What had been (at the beginning) no bigger than a full stop had expanded into a comma, a word, a sentence, a paragraph, a chapter; now it was bursting into more complex developments, becoming, one might say, a book – perhaps an encyclopaedia – even a whole language...'(*MC* 100). According to Rushdie, it is the migrant writer who is best placed to act as midwife as language itself is new-delivered; the migrant who has experienced the double loss of being 'out-of-country and out-of-language' and 'enters into an alien language' where he is 'obliged to find new ways of describing himself, new ways of being human' (*IH* 12, 278).

24

Intriguingly, Rushdie proposes Joyce as the honourable antecedent to this tradition;[60] one could perhaps add Conrad, before passing on to the familiar roll-call of 'writers from elsewhere' who have remade English for their own purposes. 'To conquer English may be to complete the process of making ourselves free' (IH 17). And English, as it happens, has proved easily accessible. In the essay 'Commonwealth Literature' Rushdie argues that if 'those peoples who were once colonized by the language are now rapidly remaking it', this is partly due to 'the English language's enormous flexibility and size', which allow newcomers to reverse the colonial process by 'carving out large territories for themselves within its frontiers' (IH 64). The 'territory' of language shares a dimension here with the contested space of the imagination. This idea is repeated in the formulation whereby books provide us with 'new and better maps of reality', 'new descriptions of the world, new maps for old' (IH 100, 202). And, if English is the world language, we should be prepared to forgo academic (or political) categorizations and recognize the novel as its world literature. 'I think that if all English literatures could be studied together, a shape would emerge which would truly reflect the new shape of the language in the world' (IH 70).

But it is not simply a matter of the English language. Rushdie celebrates what he calls the 'polyglot family tree' of the novel, citing Gogol, Cervantes, Kafka, Melville, and Machado de Assis (IH 21); and his references to Grass, Llosa, Fuentes, and Kundera remind us that it is the novel's engagement with language as such, mingling discourse within and between cultures, that is its distinguishing feature – both rhetorically and ideologically. Rushdie quotes Fuentes: 'Impose a unitary language: you kill the novel'; and in his own person he insists that the novels he values are those 'which attempt radical reformulations of language, form and ideas' – fulfilling the novel's brief 'to see the world anew' (IH 420, 393). All this is consistent with his own purpose, which has been 'to create a literary language and literary forms in which the experience of formerly colonized, still-disadvantaged peoples might find full expression' (IH 394). Rushdie's own criticism of other writers is very alert to their qualities of language,[61] and in the case of G. V. Desani (with his 1947 novel All About H. Hatterr) he acknowledges a direct influence. Desani's 'dazzling, puzzling, leaping prose is the first genuine effort to go beyond the Englishness of the English language' – not surprising, then, the admission that 'my own writing...learned a trick or two from him'.[62] It seems appropriate, therefore, that there are critics who have devoted their attention to this aspect of his work. Rustom Bharucha's essay 'Rushdie's Whale' offers an enthusiastic commentary on Rushdie's linguistic energy and inventiveness, the way he has 'bastardized... hybridized...and cinematized' the English language for his own special purposes; to stock the 'gargantuan storehouse of words' that is *Midnight's Children*, to work the subtly embroidered lexis for Rani Harappa's shawls in *Shame*. It is Bharucha's close focus on Rushdie's language that allows him to claim that 'there is a stronger emphasis [in *Shame*] on the elemental than on the political, the inexplicable rather than the rational', and to identify the imaginative world-swallowing required of the reader by Saleem Sinai as essentially a verbal exercise. 'Rarely in literature has a writer displayed a greater hunger for words, an almost frightening openness to the history of his universe'.[63] Jacqueline Bardolph's 'Language is Courage' likewise proposes that 'the courage to conceive certain thoughts, the courage of the imagination' is inherently a *linguistic* phenomenon.[64] One may take a useful critical cue (again) from James Harrison here, when he remarks that 'almost everything one can say about Rushdie's novels is exemplified in his prose style'.[65] It is to this linguistic phenomenon, this prose style, as well as to the exciting ideas and structures that they mediate, that the present study of Rushdie is addressed. And, after these necessary preliminaries, we may now return to Rushdie's own 'preliminary' novel, *Grimus*, which (reviewed as it was alongside David Lodge's *Changing Places*) set such a puzzle for his first unsuspecting readers.

2

Grimus

Rushdie's first attempt at fiction was a novel on Indian themes (called 'The Book of the Pir'), which remains unpublished; though some of the abandoned material may have found its way later into *Midnight's Children*.[1] *Grimus* represents a radically different departure. It was conceived as a contender for the Science Fiction Prize offered annually by Victor Gollancz, who published the novel; but it is hardly surprising that it was not selected as a specially successful example of the genre. Although it does have the authentic intellectual excitement associated with such fiction, and is constructed with great ingenuity, there are too many other things going on, too many other interests being served, for it to have the distinctive science-fiction polish. As we have already noted, the transgression of genre categories has remained a consistent feature of Rushdie's fiction, and this is due both to the eclectic traditions from which he has drawn and the desire – traceable to the novel's origins – to make something *new* in the world. Like his admired Fielding, Rushdie thinks of the novel (still) as a 'new province of writing',[2] and we will better understand his experimentation, the rules broken, the risks taken, and the demands made on the reader, if we share a sense of the urgency with which he persuades the novel to 'forge ... the uncreated conscience' of the reader, as Joyce had proposed to do in *A Portrait of the Artist as a Young Man* – one of the modern novels to which Rushdie most frequently alludes.[3]

Grimus is a novel about knowledge and power; about mortality and immortality; about static forms and metamorphic engines; above all, it is about the use and abuse of the human imagination. As such it engages immediately with Rushdie's major themes, perhaps prematurely and therefore in a way that cannot yet do them justice: but it has nevertheless the virtues of a young writer's confidence, daring, and uninhibited experimentation. The narrative that carries the theme echoes one of the primal fictions: the arrival of a lone man on an island, his perilous adventures among its inhabitants, his moral crisis and apotheosis. It also follows one of the elementary structural patterns, divided as it is into three parts (like Dickens's *Hard Times* and Virginia Woolf's *To the Lighthouse*; and, incidentally, Rushdie's own *Midnight's Children*): Times Past, Times Present, and Grimus. But the individual in question is no industrious Robinson Crusoe, constructing an identity as he works at his survival. Rushdie's first hero 'Flapping Eagle' is a fictional confection for our own postmodern times, a walking paradox – a white American Indian of ambivalent sexual status who has drunk an elixir of life condemning him to immortality, and who finds his way to Calf Island, somewhere in what was once the Mediterranean, in consequence of a futile suicide attempt. He has simply 'fallen through a hole in the sea' (*G.* 14) to this other half-place. We are told about Flapping Eagle's previous history in a twenty-page flashback (chapters 2–7), which details his intense relationship with a sister 'Bird-Dog' and their mutual enslavement to the magician Mr Sispy, who gives them two elixirs: 'yellow for the sun and brightness and life and blue for infinity and calm and release when I want it. Life in a yellow bottle, death blue as the sky.' Bird-Dog drinks the yellow bottle and smashes the blue one: 'Death to death.' Flapping Eagle drinks the one and keeps the other (*G.* 20–4). He becomes the lover of Livia Cramm, who tells him 'where you walk, walks Death' (*G.* 27); the contents of the blue bottle are his strength, his secret. At her death (or murder, in the complexities of the plot: they will meet again on Calf island), Flapping Eagle sets off on a symbolic voyage in her yacht – and in italics, as if to underline the elementary, pre-personal nature of his journey.

> *He was Chameleon, changeling, all things to all men and nothing to any man. He had become his enemies and eaten his friends. He was all of them and none of them.*
>
> *He was the eagle, prince of birds; and he was also the albatross. She clung round his neck and died, and the mariner became the albatross ... these were the paradoxes that swallowed him.*
>
> *A man rehearsing voices on a cliff top ... I am looking for a suitable voice to speak in.*

And after a while, he realized he had learnt nothing at all. The many, many experiences, the multitude of people and the myriad crimes had left him empty; a grin without a face. . . . He lived the same physiological day over and over again. (G. 31–3)

This is clearly to be read as a kind of proto-fiction. The impacted literary references (to Coleridge's 'Rime of the Ancient Mariner' and Hughes's *Crow* as well as to Rushdie's main bird-inspiration, Farid-ud-din 'Attar's *The Conference of the Birds*) along with the prodigality of unrealized incident prevent any real engagement in the narrative. But then Rushdie's technique is typically more demonstrative than affective. Flapping Eagle is being invested here as the first of Rushdie's mental travellers, his voyagers through remote regions of the mind, navigators of the destructive element; and the process if not the personality does therefore command our interest. This is the mode of epic rather than of psychological fiction, to which we will become attuned as we read further in Rushdie's work.

Flapping Eagle has lost the death-dealing blue bottle as Sinbad might have done, '*down a monster's throat*'; and hence the failed suicide attempt that delivers him up on the island. Calf Island, as we might expect, is no ordinary desert island either. It is a high-tech, sci-fi time zone which has more in common with Swift's Flying Island of Laputa or Blake's Island in the Moon – or any such fantastic mental structure – than with the painstaking reality of Crusoe's island with its fragile pots and precariously harvested corn. It is associated with purgatory, the medieval escape hatch from heaven and hell, via a system of references to Dante; more specifically, it has something of the Catholic theologians' consolation prize of limbo, that sterile heaven for unbaptized souls. It also has curious affinities with the mysterious mountain in Spielberg's film *Close Encounters of the Third Kind*, released the same year *Grimus* was published. Book and film share the same seventies taste for high-tech mysticism, and the kind of synthetic mythology that had been popularized by Herman Hesse in *The Glass Bead Game* and other 'anthropological' novels around this time.

The novel does, therefore, as Brennan complains, 'lack a habitus',[4] but whether this entails failure as a fiction is another matter. It presents us deliberately with a country of the mind, the collective fiction of those who have betrayed their full and frail humanity, an 'island of immortals who had found their longevity too burdensome in the outside world, yet had been unwilling to give it up' (G. 41). Fittingly, the centre of its power, and the symbol of its petrification, is the Stone Rose, conceived and created by the bird-man Grimus, Flapping Eagle's ultimate antagonist, whose name is an anagram of Simurg, the creator-bird from the Persian Book of Kings. Grimus himself, whom we meet only in Part Three, is part bird-man, part Prospero, part Pozzo/Hamm: first of those composite figures of questionable authority that Rushdie has refashioned from a 'tradition' (if it can even be called that) beginning with the oral epics and coming down to Kafka and Beckett.

But we are to meet Grimus only later. Flapping Eagle is introduced to the island by Virgil Jones, a decayed Beckettian migrant with his rocking chair and bicycle, who ironically administers the 'kiss of life' to the would-have-been suicide, recognizing in him (and revealing in himself) not so much a person as a series of literary allusions. It is Virgil Jones who gives Flapping Eagle his first lesson in plural realities, the terms of which will immediately catch the attention of readers of Rushdie's later work.

> Is it not a conceptual possibility that here, in our midst, permeating all of us and all that surrounds us, is a completely other world...? In a word, another dimension.... If you concede that conceptual possibility... you must also concede that there may well be more than one. In fact, that an infinity of dimensions might exist, as palimpsests, upon and within and around our own...' (G. 52–3)

Even Flapping Eagle protests here that he does not see the relevance of Jones's ideas to his search for his sister (which is how he himself understands his quest at this stage), anticipating the impatience of certain readers with what will appear to others as one of Rushdie's more engaging habits as a writer – his willingness to be distracted from the narrative by any stray idea that seems to offer discursive possibilities. Virgil Jones persists, introducing him to the Spiral Dancers, who had 'elevated a branch of physics until it became a high symbolist religion', and found at the heart of matter 'the pure, beautiful dance of life' – which may possibly be the first celebration in fiction of the structure of DNA (G. 75). It is Virgil Jones who has gone as far as possible, through his discipleship of Grimus himself, in creating by imaginative synthesis a viable, hospitable reality: 'With sufficient imagination, Virgil Jones had found, one could *create* worlds, physical, external worlds, neither aspects of oneself nor a palimpsest-universe. Fictions where a man could live. In those days, Mr Jones had been a highly imaginative man' (*G.* 75). It is Virgil Jones, Sancho Panza to his Don Quixote, who leads Flapping Eagle to the city of K, and to the eventual crisis of his conflict with Grimus in Part Three.

Like any mythical contender facing 'his own particular set of monsters' (*G.* 84), Flapping Eagle has to prove himself by surviving other encounters first. He has already destroyed Khallit and Mallit (*G.* 77–9), two paralysing 'extrapolations of himself' who seem with their coin-tossing ritual to have migrated from Tom Stoppard's *Rosencrantz and Guildenstern Are Dead*; he has destroyed an alter-ego constructed of his own self-doubt, and been offered ironic advice by Jones: 'You really must do something about your imagination, you know. It's so awfully lurid' (*G.* 88–9). Now, like Homer's Odysseus, or Bunyan's Christian, he must survive the temptations and distractions of the road. He must meet those who have come voluntarily, if for their different reasons to Calf Island, to follow the 'Way of K': where they 'like to think of [themselves] as complete' (*G.* 123), beyond change, beyond question. There is the beautiful Elfrida Gribb, who when suffering insomnia will 'ride through K on a small velvet donkey' (*G.* 108), locked in improbable love of her gnomelike husband Ignatius Quasimodo Gribb, one-time university professor and now author of The All-Purpose Quotable Philosophy. The moment Flapping Eagle meets her synchronizes with a 'blink', a malfunction in the intellectual system that keeps the island in being – as theologians propose that our universe depends, second by second, on God's continuous creative vigilance. The nature of the 'blink' has all the neatness of one of the technical ideas invented by Kurt Vonnegut to make his fictions work, and Rushdie handles it very cleverly – just as he juggles expertly with the different dimensions, his plural worlds themselves. He meets the 'drinking community of K' in O'Toole's bar, the Elbaroom. There is Flann Napoleon O'Toole himself ('An Irish Napoleon was a concept so grotesque it had to end up like O'Toole' (*G.* 111)), who lives in a 'haze of obscenity and vomit',

31

revelling in threats of violence, 'a masturbation of power' (G. 123). And there are his two most regular customers, One-Track Peckenpaw and Anthony StClair Peregritte-Hunte, otherwise known as The Two-Time Kid. He meets Madame Jocasta, and the distinctive girls who work in her brothel The Rising Son (sic); and 'the most beautiful man in the world', Gilles Priape. The description (and the punning name) make us observe that, among other things, *Grimus* familiarizes us with a regular feature of Rushdie's style, his addiction to what we might call the 'narrative superlative', the gratuitous hyperbole, a feature which consciously looks across to folk tale, fairy tale (and their parodic forms), rather than to the tradition of realist fiction. Indeed, the play of verbal and grammatical functions – such as the puns and anagrams indulged in here (the Gorfs actually *live* on anagrams) – are not to be dismissed as juvenile tricks, but recognized as a permanent and important aspect of Rushdie's stylistic address.

But the narrative must take its course. After a fight in the bar, where Jones is assaulted by O'Toole, Flapping Eagle goes to stay at the Gribbs' house, where he learns of his host's determination to return philosophy to the people in popular forms: 'it's all there to use, in old wives' tales, in tall stories, and most of all ... in the cliché' (G. 129). Another strand is here caught from contemporary media culture: McLuhan's *From Cliché to Archetype* had appeared in 1970. But Gribb is unwilling to enlighten Flapping Eagle about Grimus, leaving him even more determined to find out for himself 'whether he was fact or fiction' (G. 132). He is introduced to the Cherkassovs (G. 137), Aleksandr and Irina, self-exiled Russian aristocrats who are still living the revolution: 'What were we, after all, but dogs who had had their day? Night and the executioner awaited us all' (G. 139). Irina confides in Flapping Eagle that she was frozen in time when three months pregnant, her foetus 'as frozen within me as the lovers on the grecian urn' (G. 146). This prompts Jones's observation that 'Obsessionalism, "single-mindedness", the process of turning human beings into the petrified, Simplified Men of K, was a defence against the Effect' – that is, against the play of relativities that constitutes real existence (G. 149). Meanwhile, her idiot son (in another parodic Beckettian image) plays draughts with chess pieces, locked in a shed at the bottom of the garden. All these people are voluntarily trapped. They have surrendered their complexity to the Island,

and must now deny there is any other reality; or that there is a Grimus to superintend it. Only Virgil Jones and Flapping Eagle know better; only they can move about in the Dimensions. And also the sinister Nick Deggle, previously exiled from the Island (specifically to recruit Flapping Eagle: we have met him earlier, in chapter 5), but now returned, with a piece he has snapped off the Stone Rose, causing a malfunction in the reality system which is registered by the recurrent 'blink' in the narrative. Flapping Eagle's temptation by the two women represents his own 'obsession'. It is not for nothing that he is known as 'Death', because when both Irina and Elfrida fall in love with him their own fixed reality system begins to break down. As it turns out, there are to be four funerals but no wedding in this novel; and this reference to Mike Newell's popular film (from 1994) is not inappropriate, since the 'flavour of ... old films' is another element deliberately fed into the novel as part of its informed cultural perspective. As Ignatius Gribb reflects at one point, 'If he was to be in a bad Western, he might as well wear the full uniform' (G. 183, 185).

It is at this point, in Part Three, that Flapping Eagle goes in quest of Grimus himself, accompanied by Media, a whore from Jocasta's brothel with a suitably updated name who replaces Virgil Jones in the series of allusions – now playing Beatrice to his Dante. The crisis in the novel is reached when he finally meets Grimus, in the two last (and longest) chapters. In the first of these (chapter 54) the terms of the confrontation are set up – to the effect that as Flapping Eagle he is Grimus's double, with whom conflict is therefore inevitable. We learn also (from Virgil Jones's Diary) of the discovery of the Stone Rose itself, the 'geometric rose' (G. 208), by Jones and Deggle, and Grimus's dominance through his superior handling of its powers. It is Grimus who has led the other two on their 'Conceptual Travels' to the planet Thera (a transparent anagram of earth), and who names and colonizes Calf Island itself; leaving them, however, with an ontological uncertainty: 'Impossible to say whether we *found* the island or *made* it' (G. 210–11). But, if the Rose is a metaphor for the imagination, then this frozen world is an abuse of the imagination – a case of the sterile 'invention without discovery' considered in the introduction. This intellectually compromised and morally corrupt proceeding was allegorized for the nineteenth century in Tennyson's poem 'The Palace of Art'; and, as in that poem, things here start to go wrong. Deggle tries to smash Grimus's 'infernal machine', while Jones is assailed by 'an army of terrors from the recesses of my own imagination' – which Grimus puts down to 'Dimension-fever' (*G*. 216). It remains only for Liv to humiliate Flapping Eagle sexually ('breaking down the last barrier... his sexuality') before he is ready to meet Grimus on the same plane: 'he has moved from a state of what I should call self-consciousness to a state of what I would humbly term Grimus-consciousness' (*G*. 222).

The meeting takes place in Grimus's house at the top of the mountain – a mountain which is 'a model for the structure and workings of the human brain' (*G*. 232). Mountains feature regularly in Rushdie's fiction, where they are associated both with danger and with spiritual enlightenment. This association derives among other sources from the landscape of the poem *The Conference of the Birds*, and also from the story of the prophet Muhammed ascending the mountain to hear the word of God – an image that is, of course, central to *The Satanic Verses*. The house itself is an ideal construction, a 'rough triangular labyrinth' with mirrors for windows (*G*. 224–5), overtopped by the ash tree Yggdrasil (re-transplanted from Joyce's epic). Grimus has built it 'to enshrine my favourite things', especially birds: live birds, dead birds, 'an audubon proliferation of feathered heads, some real, some imaginary', centring on an image of 'the Roc of Sinbad, the Phoenix of myth: Simurg himself' (*G*. 229, 226). Alongside its function as a symbolic aviary, the house serves as a metaphor of Grimus's dissociation from the world – again, much like the situation in Tennyson's 'Palace of Art' (as Calf Island itself 'where time stood still' (*G*. 138) recalls the companion poem of withdrawal 'The Lotus Eaters'); and the moral of both poems is played out in what follows. Grimus has decided he is complete in power and wisdom and has therefore chosen to die. But, as the 'blink' reminds us, the continuing existence of the island depends, moment by moment, on his conceptualizing; and therefore he can only die like the Phoenix, which 'passes its selfhood on to its successors' (*G*. 233), to be instantly reborn in another identity. And Flapping Eagle has been selected to play this role: 'by shaping you to my grand design I remade you as completely as if you had been unmade clay'(*G*.

233). Flapping Eagle now recalls the delirious psychic voyage through alternative selves from earlier in the novel, when he was assailed by 'the memory of a man searching for a voice in which to speak' (G. 236); this was the time of his wanderings (like the Wandering Jew Ahuserius), explained now as part of Grimus's 'grand design'. But, aided by the simple presence of Media (the fearful but faithful female), Flapping Eagle resists the nomination, making the central moral accusation against Grimus for what he has done to his world, to his kind – and to himself:

> The Stone Rose has warped you, Grimus; its knowledge has made you as twisted, as eaten away by power-lust, as its effect has stunted and deformed the lives of the people you brought here.... An infinity of continua, of possibilities both present and future, the free-play of time itself, bent and shaped into a zoo for your personal enjoyment. (G. 236)

Grimus alludes in the course of their conversation to his own past, one that includes wars, prison camps, torture, and execution – sufficiently emblematic of twentieth-century history; this is what he has turned aside from, as Flapping Eagle perceives, 'away from the world, into books and philosophies and mythologies, until these became his realities...and the world was just an awful nightmare' (G. 243). But even this is no excuse for abandoning his humanity. 'You are so far removed from the pains and torments of the world you left and the world you made that you can even see death as an academic exercise' (G. 236).

As part of the prepared ritual of his death, Grimus (now 'the ancient infant', in an imagined process of continuous reversal that recalls Blake's poem 'The Mental Traveller') and Flapping Eagle are fused into one identity. The passage is rendered in Rushdie's most dense philosophic style:

> Self. My self. Myself and he alone. Myself and his self in the glowing bowl. Yes, it was like that. Myself and himself pouring out of ourselves into the glowing bowl....My son. The mind of Grimus rushing to me. You are my son, I give you my life. *I have become you, I have become you are me.*...The mandarin monk released into me in an orgasm of thinking....Like a beating of wings his self flying in. *My son, my son, what father fathered a son like this, as I do in my sterility.* (G. 242–3)

One answer to Grimus's rhetorical question might be Victor Frankenstein, who fathered his own 'son' in the sterility of his scientific ambition. Immortality and sterility go together on Calf Island, and the perversion of the procreative process – Mary Shelley's own nightmare theme – is part of Grimus's dehumanizing programme. Assuming his new powers, Flapping Eagle travels to Thera, to be instructed by the Gorf, Dota (whose comments on Grimus's abuse of the Rose puncture any excessive solemnity: *'It is a flagrant distortion of Conceptual Technology to use the Rose to Conceptualize... coffee'* (G. 245)). Grimus is brutally murdered by O'Toole's gang (again as part of his own design), and his body burnt along with the symbolic ash tree and its complement of mythological birds. It remains to be seen how the new composite self of 'I-Eagle' will react. But, in the final moment of crisis, he maintains his resistance to the sterilizing, simplifying ideas of his mentor/maker: 'The combined force of unlimited power, unlimited learning, and a rarefied, abstract attitude to life which exalted these two into the greatest goals of humanity, was a force I-Eagle could not bring himself to life' (G. 251). He eliminates the Stone Rose ('No, I-Eagle thought, the Rose is not the supreme gift'), and Calf Mountain unmakes itself, 'its molecules and atoms breaking, dissolving, quietly vanishing into primal, unmade energy. The raw material of being was claiming its own' (G. 251–3).

And one of these primal energies is sexual. Significantly, the overthrow of Grimus is celebrated by the eventual coupling of Flapping Eagle and Media, the 'orgasm of thinking' replaced by sexual orgasm, our own ordinary (but also extraordinary) means of access to the other, to the future, and to our own true fulfilment: to all we know, and all we need to know on earth (perhaps) of transcendence. There is some doubt as to how one might interpret the end of the novel. The sexual solution with Media has a strongly positive note, as if his and her identity are salvaged in human terms. But we might equally understand that Flapping Eagle dissolves along with Calf Island itself as a result of his encounter with Grimus; as the price of his 'human' victory. (After all, we might risk the simple question: where would he have to go?) It is instructive to compare this ambiguous situation with the 'dissolution' of the narrator Saleem Sinai at the end of *Midnight's Children*: is this a metaphor or is it a 'real' fictional death? The very terms in which one puts the question reveal that it makes no difference to the resolution of the theme. But even here, one should note that the 'relation' between Grimus and Flapping Eagle is itself ambiguous. On the one hand, Grimus is the author of Eagle's metamorphoses, his immortality, his access to an infinite number of alternative selves: like a beneficent creator. But, on the other hand, he has only put him through this 'apprenticeship' in order to prepare him for the assumption of Grimus's own role, as the tyrant of being, the One, the Overmind (or over-artist). So the benefits of plural being are offset by the threat (the certainty) of the petrification of his humanity through the power of the Stone Rose. This makes *Grimus* the first of Rushdie's allegorical representations of the recurrent opposition between the many and the one; and, clearly enough, a dress rehearsal for the more recognizable materials lined up against each other – inside each other – in *The Satanic Verses*. (There is even an elision of angel/devil to ponder on: G. 31.) Grimus is a secular Imam; Grimus's frozen time is the equivalent of the 'untime of the Imam' in the later novel, the establishment of a fixed, sacral eternity over the flexibility and fallibility of human time.

Grimus is a young man's novel; it is ambitious, over-literary, philosophically overheated; a 'novel of ideas' in the doubtful sense that it is the ideas that run the show. It is in this sense that it may be considered 'premature'. But it is also brilliant in its design and successful in many of its devices; and if the ideas run the show they are at least absorbing ideas.[5] Rushdie himself did the novel a disservice by conceding in one early interview that it was 'too clever for its own good'; better a book that is too clever than one that is not clever enough. Reviewing his fiction to date in a later interview, however, as a 'body of work', he is prepared to allow *Grimus* its proper place: 'I also see my first novel...as part of this. Metaphysical concerns were present in a different way in the first novel.'[6] It is not so much unfortunate as inappropriate, therefore, that some of Rushdie's critics have chosen to denounce the novel gravely as a failure. Brennan's schoolmasterly tone ('this parable of crude acculturation'...'the stance of complacent philosophical scepticism'), and Catherine Cundy's description of a 'chaotic fantasy with no immediately discernible arguments of any import' both choose to ignore the novel's essential humanism and high spirits.[7] But the unprejudiced reader will stand a good chance of finding these out for him or herself.

3

Midnight's Children

One thousand and one, Rushdie reminds us halfway through *Midnight's Children*, is 'the number of night, of magic, of alternative realities' (*MC* 212). And the novel is a modern odyssey, an epic navigation through these alternative realities: myth and history, memory and document, moonlight and daylight; the refractions of art, the centripetal and centrifugal dynamics of the self; the babel of languages, the alternating (and competing) religious and political understandings of the world. The challenge of Rushdie's project is to create a fiction that does justice to these multiple realities, bringing them together in a way that allows each strand a voice, a presence, without obliterating the others. Saleem Sinai refers at one point to the 'two threads' of his narrative, 'the thread that leads to the ghetto of the magicians; and the thread that tells the story of Nadir the rhymeless, verbless poet' (*MC* 46), but, although these are indeed central strands, the weave is much richer and more various than this phrase would suggest.

The basic narrative strategy is simple: the juxtaposition of the public and the private, the historical and the biographical – in what is, after all, a time-honoured technique, to be found in Plutarch, Shakespeare and Walter Scott as well as in Rushdie's modern exemplars. And so the 'birth-of-a-nation' theme in the novel is parallelled by the strictly synchronized birth of the central character (and first-person narrator) Saleem Sinai, representative as he is of the 1,001 magical children supposed to have been born in that historical hour after the declaration of independence by Jarwhal Nehru at the midnight before 15 August 1947. (Rushdie has since calculated that, in demographical fact, at two births per second, around 7,000 children would actually have been born during this time; so his magical number turns out to be 'a little on the low side' (*IH* 26).) And the mode of narration is (or appears to be) equally straightforward and well tried: Saleem tells his story to a simple woman, Padma, as they work together in the pickle factory that provides both a refuge for them at the end of the narrative and a metaphor for the fictional process itself. It is worth recalling, therefore, that the novel began as a third-person 'omniscient' narrative, and threatened to become engulfed in its materials until Rushdie hit upon the idea of the narrator/narratee, which had the effect of both lightening and focusing these same materials.[1] It was a fortunate solution; as many readers have testified, it is the relationship between Padma and Saleem, made up of her interruptive comments and his evasions, that provides our point of entry into the novel, and sustains our interest through its many complications. (Although it should be said the relationship has been read more critically from a post-colonial standpoint, as exemplifying the patronizing exploitation of the indigenous working class by a condescending cosmopolitan author.)[2]

The relationship between the written and the spoken word is a matter of ancient debate, and one question that arises within it is how the novel can ever encompass orality: how much sense it makes for Sterne to claim, for example, that writing is 'but a different name for conversation'.[3] This has been the focus of much of the commentary on *Midnight's Children*. But, whatever view we take of the evident artificiality of the conversation between Saleem and Padma, it does allow Rushdie to develop a narrative inflection which becomes characteristic – almost a signature – from this point on. This is a process we might call 'tessellation', after the way tiles are laid to overlap on a roof, whereby the narrative is always looping back in recapitulation, and also looking forward ('proleptically') in anticipation. The effect is to bring a depth of field to the present moment, creating an impression of simultaneity and temporal suspension – as the fluid present, the elusive *now*, is always pressed on by the past and foreshadowed, drawn forward into the future. Saleem describes himself at one point as writing at the apex of an isosceles triangle, where past and present meet (*MC* 191); but the projection into the future is also part of the fictional geometry. One wonders, indeed, whether this is one reason that the thirty chapters are not numbered – almost as if they could be shuffled around and read in any order (as is the design of Julio Cortazar's novel *Hopscotch*[4]) – so self-contained and interwoven is each of them, reproducing (like the genetic code) the essential information of the novel. Thus, perched in the middle of his novel at the 'Alpha and Omega' chapter [16], Saleem announces 'my story's half-way point', looking both back and forwards: 'there are beginnings here, and all manner of ends' (*MC* 218). And, just as we have already visited the end of the story ('It is morning at the pickle-factory; they have brought my son to see me...Someone speaks anxiously, trying to force her way into my story ahead of time'(*MC* 205)), so when we approach the actual conclusion the earlier scenes are recycled. The first two pages of 'A Wedding' [chapter 28] are a good example; Saleem can explain to Padma his marriage to Parvati-the-Witch only by linking this back to the story of all the women in his life, beginning (again) in 'a blind landowner's house on the shores of a Kashmiri lake', with Naseem Aziz his unmarried grandmother (*MC* 391–2). 'Once upon a time'; 'I have told this story before' (*MC* 209, 212, 354); the phrases borrowed from oral narrative recur like a refrain through the novel, animating its texture.

Let us return to the structure of juxtapositions. Saleem is born at midnight on 15 August 1947 – 'at the precise instant of India's arrival at independence, I tumbled forth into the world' (*MC* 11) – and throughout the novel the threads are carefully cross-stitched. In the chapter [14] 'My Tenth Birthday', 'freak weather – storms, floods, hailstones from a cloudless sky – ...managed to wreck the second Five Year Plan;' – this on the very day Saleem founds 'my very own M.C.C....the new Midnight Children's Conference' (*MC* 202–3). He uses newspaper cuttings from the year 1960 to compose the fatal communication to Commander Sabarmati revealing his wife's affair, and confesses to this as 'my first attempt at rearranging history' (*MC* 252–3). The underlying principle, or logic, is restated several times in the conversational ebb and flow of the address, but nowhere more explicitly than at the beginning of [chapter 17] 'The Kolynos Kid'. Here Saleem offers to 'amplify, in the manner and with the proper solemnity of a man of science, my claim to a place at the centre of things' (*MC* 232). In a historical character the claim would be preposterous; for a fictional narrator it is a truism, a condition of his being at all. 'I was linked to history both literally and metaphorically, both actively and passively, in what our (admirably modern) scientists might term "modes of connection" composed of "dualistically-combined configurations" of the two pairs of opposed adverbs given above' (*MC* 232). Without agreeing with his position (which is typically exclusive), one can see what Timothy Brennan means when he says that Rushdie is 'best seen as a critic' rather than as a novelist at all, since his novels are so uncompromisingly metafictional; they are not so much (he says) novels in themselves as 'novels about Third-World novels'.[5] But the irony of Saleem's 'claims' need not have such a distancing or alienating effect. Indeed, this is how Rushdie conducts the delicate negotiation between fact and fiction in the novel, which has been well described by Andrzej Gasiorek:

> *Midnight's Children* is . . . a double-voiced narrative in which a personal discourse of self-discovery interacts with, and is constrained by, a public discourse of history and politics. . . . [it] persistently admonishes those who either succumb to private fantasies about the world or distort it for political purposes. . . . Rushdie's narrative mode does not seek to do away with the distinction between fantasy and reality but shows how strange and unstable was the political reality of the time.[6]

It is in these terms that we have to read the chapter [21] 'Drainage and Desert', as an elaborate but also ironic correspondence between Saleem's own life story so far and the progress of the Indo-Chinese border war of 1962 (*MC* 286–7). Likewise, we are invited to believe that 'the hidden purpose of the Indo-Pakistani war of 1965 was nothing more nor less than the elimination of my benighted family from the face of the earth' (*MC* 327). Saleem is drawn to conflict: 'the belligerent events of 1971', the civil war in Pakistan, deliver him up as a guide in the Pakistani army; prompting his disappearance in to the Sundarbans and his reappearance seven months later into 'the world of armies and dates' (*MC* 356). India's first nuclear explosion in May 1974 coincides pointedly with the return of the warlike Shiva (Saleem's anti-self) into the narrative, while the painfully protracted labour of Parvati to deliver her child Aadam parallels the period of thirteen days in June 1975 between the returning of the guilty verdict on Mrs Gandhi and her seizure of emergency powers (*MC* 420–4). Saleem himself becomes a victim of the compulsory sterilization programme adopted under these powers, providing a final metaphor for the expunging of the hope of the Indian people – 'sperectomy' – at the hands of certain Indian politicians.

The problematic terms of the relationship between history and lived experience are deliberately brought into question by Rushdie through the factual errors introduced into the narrative – which may be understood as a kind of immunization, for the reader, against too uncritical a reading. Rushdie's own essay 'Unreliable Narration in *Midnight's Children*' considers this very question: how, 'using memory as our tool . . . we remake the past to suit our present purposes'. His hero's story is in this sense exemplary: 'The reading of Saleem's unreliable narration might be . . . a useful analogy for the way in which we all, every day, attempt to "read" the world' (*IH* 24–5). In the novel itself he confesses that 're-reading my work, I have discovered an error in chronology. The assassination of Mahatma Gandhi occurs, in these pages, on the wrong date.' And this cannot now be corrected: 'in my India, Gandhi will continue to die at the wrong time' (*MC* 164). Of course, in a sense the assassination will always have been 'at the wrong time', and the reader is expected to pick up on this; but the error prompts the narrator's question: 'Does one error invalidate the entire fabric? Am I so far gone, in my desperate need for meaning, that I'm prepared to distort everything – to rewrite the whole history of my times purely in order to place myself in a central role?' (*MC* 164). It is left for the reader to judge – this is his right and his 'responsibility', to use the term from Keith Wilson's essay.[7] But the implicit answer is no, because there is always more to history than the facts. ('Some legends make reality, and become more useful than the facts' (*MC* 47).)

We do have to 'build reality' from scraps of information (*MC* 412), and *Midnight's Children* is solidly built of facts and figures, dates and events, that are incontrovertible: from Amritsar, Bangladesh, and Bhopal to Queen Victoria, two world wars and General Zia. But the story we end up with will always be conditional, 'open at both ends'. If 'reality is question of perspective' (*MC* 164) – an axiom that also galvanizes *Gulliver's Travels* – then the perspective of a living observer (and participant) will always be changing, switching between the two poles of a supposedly subjective or ostensibly objective standpoint. This, we should remember, is how the imagination works; and we have been warned against its capacity for error and distortion. The subjective view is unreliable for two reasons: owing to the fallibility of both our perceptions and our memories. Our perceptions to start with are subject to the moment-by-moment fluctuations of consciousness. Although Rushdie is not to be described as a psychological novelist in the manner of Joyce or Virginia Woolf, in that his own narrative point of view is typically epic and externalized ('must we look', asks Saleem, 'beyond psychology' (*MC* 143)), he is nevertheless acutely aware of the unpredictability of our cognitive processes and the fragility of 'the mind's divisions between fantasy and reality' (*MC* 165). We have seen how this was a central theme of *Grimus*, and it will provide a major preoccupation of *The Satanic Verses*; but (as the quotation just given indicates) it is a minor theme of *Midnight's Children* as well. The macro-scale of history is always related back to the micro-scale of the individual. 'Religion was the glue of Pakistan,' we are told in [chapter 24] 'The Buddha', 'holding the halves together'; and then the analogy is immediately made with consciousness: 'just as consciousness, the awareness of oneself as a homogeneous entity in time, a blend of past and present, is the glue of personality, holding together our then and our now' (*MC* 341). The historical epic scene must always contain the personal lyric self.

The deposit of perception and experience in the memory introduces another variable, because the memory has its own transforming function: it 'selects, eliminates, alters, exaggerates, minimizes, glorifies, and vilifies', and in so doing it 'creates its own reality, its heterogeneous but usually coherent version of events' (*MC* 207). Coherent within its own terms, we may notice, rather than reliably correspondent to any external scheme of things; we might reasonably invoke the philosophers' use of precisely these terms to describe alternative epistemological systems. It is worth noting, also, the closeness of this description of the memory to that Rushdie gives of the imagination in an essay quoted above, in Chapter 1 (p. 10). It is the powerful but unpredictable functioning of these faculties that makes us human beings, with all our dangerous potential for good and evil, rather than behavioural automata or cyberpets. The aggregation of these subjectivities on the demographic scale introduces another level of unreality, beyond the memorial grasp of any individual. 'Futility of statistics: during 1971, ten million refugees fled across the borders of East Pakistan–Bangladesh into India – but ten million (like all numbers larger than one thousand and one) refuses to be understood' (*MC* 346). What Rushdie refers to elsewhere as 'all this cold history' (*MC* 186) means nothing unless warmed, brought to life, by the individual consciousness.

The conclusion that is borne in upon us is that a history is put together, invented, by a people, just as a person is invented by circumstance (and as a character is invented in a novel). The creation of India itself, celebrated in the chapter [8] 'Tick, Tock', its coming into being at a designated moment in time, is a 'mass fantasy', a 'new myth', a 'collective fiction':

> because a nation which had never previously existed was about to win its freedom, catapulting us into a world which, although it had five thousand years of history, although it had invented the game of chess and traded with Middle Kingdom Egypt, was nevertheless quite imaginary; into a mythical land, a country which would never exist except by the efforts of a phenomenal collective will – except in a dream we all agreed to dream... (*MC* 111)

And if we draw the focus back further, from historical time to mythical time, we achieve yet another dislocation in our perspective. Talking to Saleem's grandfather Aadam Aziz, Tai the boatman claims 'an antiquity so immense it defied numbering'; his 'magical talk' derives from 'the most remote Himalayas of the past': 'I have watched the mountains being born; I have seen Emperors die' (*MC* 16–17). The prehistorical Bombay of the fishermen is invoked 'at the dawn of time... in this primeval world before clocktowers' (*MC* 92). And even as Saleem recalls the moment of his birth, made so significant by its coincidence with that of his country, he then locates this moment in the 'long time' of Hindu myth to provide a vertiginous sense of 'the dark backward and abysm of time':[8]

> Think of this: history, in my version, entered a new phase on August 15th, 1947 – but in another version, that inescapable date is no more than one fleeting instant in the Age of Darkness, Kali-Yuga... [which] began on Friday, February 18th, 3102 B.C; and will last a mere 432,000 years! Already feeling somewhat dwarfed, I should add nevertheless that the Age of Darkness is only the fourth phase of the

present Maha-Yuga cycle which is, in total, ten times as long; and when you consider that it takes a thousand Maha-Yugas to make just one Day of Brahma, you'll see what I mean about proportion. (*MC* 191)

Now: the ambivalent status of this 'collective fantasy' will obviously reflect on the ability of the artist (as well as the historian) to represent it. And this is where we can move on from an account of the parallel structure of *Midnight's Children* to consider the nature of the fictional discourse itself.

Interestingly (and – as is made clear from reading his later work – typically), Rushdie provides several surrogate portraits of the artist within the novel, each of whom contributes in some way to the metafictional level; that is, the commentary within the text on artistic problems and procedures. The first of these is Tai the boatman (who has been introduced above), a kind of Charon figure, also described as a 'watery Caliban, rather too fond of cheap Kashmiri brandy' (*MC* 16). Tai will not be taxed as to his *real* age, any more than Haroun's father (later) will tell only *true* stories; that is not the point. And he is, of course, illiterate: 'literature crumbled beneath the rage of his sweeping hand' (*MC* 17). From his 'magical words' Aadam Aziz learns 'the secrets of the lake' (*MC* 18), and much else besides. A demotic Tiresias, Tai is as old as memory itself – the embodiment of the oral tradition, and the source of all storytelling. But where there is no claim, no provocation, there is no artistic hubris, no transgression; Tai is as innocent in this exchange as at his death (significantly, at the hands of partitionist fanatics). But we soon hear of a painter with more questionable aims, 'whose paintings had grown larger and larger as he tried to get the whole of life into his art' (*MC* 48) – and who commits suicide out of disappointment. Later on, Lifafa Das the peep-show man presents a similar case. He has his promotional patter: '"Come see everything, come see everything, come see! Come see Delhi, come see India, come see" ... "see the whole world, come see everything!"' Das reminds Saleem of Nadir Khan's friend the painter, and he asks himself 'is this an Indian disease, this urge to encapsulate the whole of reality? Worse: am I infected, too?' (*MC* 73–5). His scriptwriter uncle Hanif provides another example, as he turns his back on myth and fantasy in favour of social realism.

'Sonny Jim,' he informed me, 'this damn country has been dreaming for five thousand years. It's about time it started waking up.' Hanif was fond of railing against princes and demons, gods and heroes, against, in fact, the entire iconography of the Bombay film; in the temple of illusions, he had become the high priest of reality... (*MC* 237)

Hanif's realism is no less questionable than any other representation; and there is an ironic self-reference in that Hanif's latest script concerns 'the Ordinary Life of a Pickle Factory' (*MC* 236), guying the very metaphoric *locus* where Rushdie's novel will end. Even Saleem's old friend Picture Singh, the snake-charmer from the magicians' ghetto, is humbled by a heckler's gibe during his performance 'which had questioned the hold on reality which was his greatest pride' (*MC* 399). In each case, the artist here has tried to claim a franchise on reality which is untenable. The limitless 'real' may be enticed by the 'true', but it can never be contained by it. Tai the boatman would have known better.

Saleem-as-author has himself confessed to these irreverent imaginings. He succumbs to the belief that 'I was somehow creating a world', where real people 'acted at my command': 'which is to say, I had entered into the illusion of the artist, and thought of the multitudinous realities of the land as the raw unshaped material of my gift' (*MC* 172). He does have some excuse for his 'self-aggrandizement' here, in that, 'if I had not believed myself in control of the flooding multitudes, their massed identities would have annihilated mine.' The fact that this is precisely what happens at the end of the novel establishes another self-reflexive commentary: the artist cannot, in the end, stand against either the tide or the dust of history. And so what are presented as Saleem's 'problems with reality' (*MC* 421) approximate to Rushdie's own. In the last chapter, as 'an infinity of new endings clusters round my head' – including Padma's conventional happy ending – he has to resist the seductions of fantasy, of *mere* imagining. More insistent even than Padma, 'reality is nagging at me'. And, because of his response to this, his thirty picklejar chapters preserve 'the authentic taste of truth' (*MC* 428, 444). The taste of truth: it is an interesting formula. A formula for fiction, where (as Saleem remarks earlier) 'what's real and what's true aren't necessarily the same': '*True*, for me, was from my earliest days something hidden inside the stories Mary Pereira told me' (*MC* 79). We cannot 'produce' reality to order, but we can recognize the truth, in what is a complex act of moral and imaginative recognition. This is a truth which neither requires 'evidence', nor is undermined by the discourse of 'magic realism' into which the narrative frequently switches. This gives us blood that falls as rubies, tears as diamonds; and the whole chapter ([14] 'My Tenth Birthday') on the miraculous qualities of the midnight children themselves. 'To anyone whose personal cast of mind is too inflexible to accept these facts, I have this to say: That's how it was; there can be no retreat from the truth' (*MC* 194).

And this is in the end how the novel defends itself, and establishes its own integrity. Not by protestation: there can be 'no proof' of the fact that Naseem 'eavesdropped on her daughters' dreams' (*MC* 56), nor of the sterilization of the midnight children: the evidence 'went up in smoke' (*MC* 424). Rushdie could repeat Sidney's celebrated axiom: 'for the poet, he nothing affirms, and therefore never lieth.'[9] And in a sense he does so, when he claims that literature is 'self-validating' (*IH* 14); validated by what Wordsworth appealed to in his 'Preface to the *Lyrical Ballads*' as that 'truth which is its own testimony', the internal evidence of art itself.'[10] And this 'evidence' is provided by the confidence with which, in *Midnight's Children*, the different discourses are allowed to play alongside and against each other, the wonderful free-style of the narration – more cursive than coercive – that draws as it needs from a miscellany of styles and modes. It is this confidence that allows Rushdie to use the double-sided, reversible formula from oral tradition – 'I was in the basket, but also not in the basket' (*MC* 368) – which is more systematically invoked as the imaginative axis of *The Satanic Verses*, but plays its relevant part here. It is the formula that asserts nothing, that leaves everything suspended in the light wind of fictional hypothesis; that can build on sand, on water (like Dr Narlikar's tetrapods), or maintain itself in the air. It is this confidence that gives Rushdie access to that fictive plenitude, that generosity of vision and prodigality of incarnation that is best described (in its generic aspect) by Mikhail Bakhtin, and by critics who operate on a Bakhtinian wavelength.[11]

The very metaphor of the 'wavelength' reminds us of a specially important means of access to fictive plenitude in the novel: not just the radio itself, key though it is to the operation of the Midnight Children's Conference, but telecommunications generally, both as instrument and image. The instrumentality of telecommunications is underlined by the narrator himself, as Saleem recommends his 'future exegetes' to consider the intervention of 'a single unifying force. I refer to telecommunications. Telegrams, and after telegrams, telephones, were my undoing' (*MC* 287). Not only Saleem's undoing, we may add. The telephone plays a sinister part in many of Rushdie's fictions: 'squat at the ear of Eve, familiar toad', in the Miltonic phrase, it replaces the serpent as the contemporary tempter, equivocator, and general conduit of evil. Edenic possibilities in both *The Satanic Verses* and *The Moor's Last Sigh* are also destroyed by it. In *Midnight's Children* it is over the telephone that Saleem's mother gives away the secret of her meetings with ex-husband Nadir, and that Lila Sabarmati betrays her adulterous liaison – bringing about three deaths. The mass media play their part as well. Saleem's birth is announced in the newspaper, and many of the historical events in the novel are brought to us over the radio. Disdaining old-fashioned omniscience, this narrator prefers to use more modern forms of mediation; a feature that adds to the plurality of voices through which the novel is articulated. And this exploitation of the media is on reflection unsurprising, when we think, for example, of how Marshall McLuhan welcomed them in the 1960s as 'the extensions of man', the elaboration of our very nervous system – bringing with them a new definition of consciousness. (The fact that McLuhan makes a parodic appearance in *Grimus* – as he did, in person, in Woody Allen's film *Annie Hall* – underlines the convergence of ideas.) Dickens, we know, turned newspapers to good account in the middle of the previous century: what more refractions of his world might he not have offered us via radio and television? And it was Kipling, another celebrated journalist, who was one of the first to bring the modern media into fiction, with his stories 'Mrs Bathhurst' (where the plot centres on a fragment of remembered film) and 'Wireless' (on the quasi-mystical seductions of early, pre-regulation radio broadcasts).[12] Does this represent another debt owed by Rushdie to those he has already acknowledged to the author of *Kim*? As the chapter [12] 'All-India Radio' explains, the telepathic radio also functions as the

main line of communication between the midnight children –
with Saleem as the sensitive receiver. To begin with, the voices
assail him as 'a headful of gabbling tongues, like an untuned
radio', but he soon learns to use the new instrument:

> By sunrise, I had discovered that the voices could be controlled – I
> was a radio receiver, and could turn the volume down or up; I could
> select individual voices; I could even, by an effort of will, switch off
> my newly-discovered inner ear. It was astonishing how soon fear left
> me; by morning, I was thinking, 'Man, this is better than All-India
> Radio, man; better than Radio Ceylon!' (*MC* 161–2)

He even goes so far, later, as to complain that he seems to be
'stuck with this radio metaphor' (*MC* 221); as indeed he is, until
the untimely sinus operation deprives him of his special gift.

But, as we might expect, in a verbal art form that aspires to the
pictorial; that strains, as Joseph Conrad urged it should, to make
us *see*, it is the visual media that offer themselves most readily
for metaphoric elaboration. Early on, Saleem plays such
variations on his 'memory of a mildewed photograph' of his
father Aadam Aziz shaking hands with Mian Abdullah (the
Hummingbird), with the formidable Rani of Cooch Naheen in
the background. The photograph is not simply 'described'; it is
milked of its visuality to provide a soundtrack ('there is a
conversation going on in the photograph'), an interpretation of
a key phase in Indian politics of the 1930s ('Beyond the door,
history calls' (*MC* 45)). Photography is used elsewhere; we meet
a '*Times of India* staff photographer, who was full of sharp tales
and scurrilous stories' (*MC* 240), and it is an Eastman-Kodak
portrait that provides 'Picture Singh' with his nickname (*MC*
368). But it is film that provides more dynamic images for the
novel. It was not just for effect that Rushdie once claimed in an
interview that the films of Buñuel had had more influence on
him as a writer than the work of James Joyce; and it is the
cinema above all that provides him with a reference point, an
adaptable metaphor for the manipulation of point of view. This
is how he describes his spying through the window on the
meetings of his mother, Amina, and her one-time husband
Nadir Khan in the Pioneer Cafe: 'what I'm watching here on my
dirty glass cinema-screen is, after all, an Indian movie...' (*MC*
212–13). And (in an often-quoted passage), the processes of

perception and retrospection themselves are interpreted via the cinema screen.

> Reality is a question of perspective; the further you get from the past, the more concrete and plausible it seems – but as you approach the present, it inevitably seems more and more incredible. Suppose yourself in a large cinema, sitting at first in the back row, and gradually moving up, row by row, until your nose is almost pressed against the screen. Gradually the stars' faces dissolve into dancing grain; tiny details assume grotesque proportions; the illusion dissolves – or rather, it becomes clear that the illusion itself *is* reality... (*MC* 164)

Rushdie quotes the passage in his essay 'Imaginary Homelands' to make the point that we cannot hope to see the present clearly, as a 'whole picture'; there will be inevitable distortion (*IH* 13). One might remark here that there is an unhappy irony in the fact that Rushdie and other interested parties have encountered insuperable difficulties in attempting to bring this most filmable of novels to the screen. The governments of both India and Sri Lanka have refused to provide locations for the film, allegedly for fear of alienating Muslim communities. And as Rushdie has observed: you cannot construct Bombay in a studio.[13]

It is curious, in this connection, that Timothy Brennan chooses to take Rushdie to task for his use of the media, suggesting that this is another instance of ideological compromise, a sell-out to Western values – as defined by 'the media and the market'. Rushdie is accused of 'historicizing events without processing them...in the manner of the media', and of responding to events according to 'the way in which the news and media desensitise our response'. He is seen by this critic as being complicit in the process whereby '"native" or local culture seems to be rendered meaningless by a communications network that effortlessly crosses borders and keeps an infinite stock of *past* artistic styles'; and – finally – as investing in that 'crossbreeding of market and media' which 'produces an inhuman blob, as faceless as it is powerful.'[14] Andrzej Gasiorek, by contrast, argues that Rushdie stands *outside* the frame of his media references, offering a critique of rather than a collaboration with their operations (which is surely the case: one has only to think of the savage satire of the news media in chapter [23] 'How Saleem Achieved Purity'; the 'divorce between news

50

and reality', the 'mirages and lies' (*MC* 323-4)); and Steven Connor goes so far as to propose that it is the interface of prose fiction with the electronic media which provides the very grain and substance/quality of Rushdie's vision. 'Rushdie exploits the forms and resources of the medium of radio, along with those of film and, in later novels... of television and video, because such forms are the evidence of a fundamentally new relationship between public and private life.' If the realist novel, says Connor, explored the *differentiation* of public and private, 'by contrast the forms of contemporary mass culture bring about a mutual permeation of the private and public, such that the integrity of both is dissolved and a relationship of difference is no longer possible between them'.[15] This is McLuhan's prophecy restated as cultural fact, and as such the observation offers a valuable comment on how Rushdie's fiction actually works.

But there is another important theme which we have touched on only glancingly so far, which requires further consideration at the end of this chapter. This is the theme of birth itself – announced in the very first sentence – which functions as the central metaphor of the novel, generating everything else. It is, after all, and axiomatically, through birth that *newness enters the world*; and it is through a complex and elaborated system of metaphors of birth and rebirth that Rushdie moves from merely physical propagation outwards to psychological, cultural, and political formations. It is also worth remarking that this is the most relevant context of his debt to Sterne, because it is the generative, obstetrical, and pediatric imagery in *Tristram Shandy* that provides a model for Rushdie's own exploration of these ideas. A good deal of critical attention has been lavished on the theme of problematic parentage in Rushdie,[16] which is understandable, since it recurs in all his novels and is (he himself reminds us) an important circumstance in both the *Mahabharata* and the *Ramayana*, the founding epics of India. But the fact of birth itself – what cannot occur, we remember, on Calf Island – is for Rushdie a much more powerful and pervasive idea, providing the ground for metaphors of rebirth also, which may actually be invested with greater symbolic power (as Robinson Crusoe's rebirth onto his desert island, when he is delivered up by a wave from 'deep in its own body',[17] is more eloquent than the bald birth announcement in the novel's first sentence).

51

Midnight's Children is unambiguously a nativity novel. It begins with Saleem Sinai's own birth announcement, and ends not with a death (or even a marriage) but with the dissolution of that single citizen of India and his unique identity into the mass, the undifferentiated energies of the new and always renewable nation. Rushdie has commented on this ending: 'The story of Saleem does indeed lead him to despair. But the story is told in a manner designed to echo, as closely as my abilities allowed, the Indian talent for non-stop regeneration' (*IH* 16). The actual moment of Saleem's birth, in the countdown chapter [8] 'Tick, Tock', is related as a lyrical counterpoint between Amina's accelerating contractions and the birth of India itself: 'The monster in the streets has already begun to celebrate; the new myth courses through its veins, replacing its blood with corpuscles of saffron and green' (*MC* 114). It is significant that this scene and its attendant circumstances are revisited throughout the novel: Dr Narlikar's Bombay Nursing Home is one of its key locations. Not the least reason for this, of course, is that it is here that Mary Pereira switches the two newborn boys, so that Saleem (who is actually the child of the serving-woman Vanita and the Englishman William Methwold) is brought up to a life of privilege by Shiva's biological parents, Amina and Ahmed Sinai; meanwhile, Shiva becomes the street-bred criminal and militarist, Saleem's ordained opposite.[18] And there are also other births recorded: not only the 'collective birth' of the midnight children themselves, but the births of parents, siblings, cousins, children, in a kind of fertility ritual that serves to contradict the infamous sterilization programme of the 'Green Witch' Indira Gandhi, and to suggest the adoption of one sentence from the novel as its epigraph: 'no new place is real until it has seen a birth' (*MC* 102). One filament of the birth theme is taken up in the metaphor of the perforated sheet that appears at the end of the first chapter, where Dr Aziz is invited to examine his future wife through 'a crude circle about seven inches in diameter' cut in a sheet held by two women (*MC* 23). The hole in the sheet develops into a complex metaphor for our access via the perforated hymen to the place of conception and the avenue of birth, and eventually through life to death, via the last exit of the pyre or the tomb. But the sheet also suggests the circumscription of our perceptions themselves (as it functioned literally for Dr Aziz); and the 'pointillist', accumulative process necessary to build these into a coherent vision and narrative. As such, it provides a central point (or gap?) of reference, to which Rushdie frequently recurs: as when his sister Jamila Singer performs in public behind a perforated veil (*MC* 304), or where Saleem's grandmother appears to him, 'staring down through the hole in a perforated cloud, waiting for my death so that she could weep a monsoon for forty days' (*MC* 444).

But it is possible to locate a more specific reference even to the moment of conception itself, lodged at the centre of the most mysterious chapter in *Midnight's Children*: [25] 'In the Sundarbans'. This chapter is in some respects the key to the novel, in that it homes in on the principle of transformability/metamorphosis – performing a function not unlike the visit to the Cave of Spleen in book IV of Pope's *Rape of the Lock*: another Ovidian excursus from the social–historical plane. Rushdie made some very interesting comments on this section of the novel in his interview with John Haffenden:

> if you are going to write an epic, even a comic epic, you need a descent into hell. That chapter is the inferno chapter, so it was written to be different in texture from what was around it. Those were among my favourite ten or twelve pages to write, and I was amazed at how they divided people so extremely.[19]

In this chapter the man-dog Saleem (known at this stage as 'Buddha' because of his taciturnity) deserts from the Pakistani army into which he has been recruited as a tracker, along with the three young soldiers he is meant to be guiding, 'into the historyless anonymity of rain-forests' (*MC* 349), effectively deserting the historical surface of the fiction for another, atavistic plane: 'an overdose of reality gave birth to a miasmic longing for flight into the safety of dreams.' Not that dreams are necessarily safe places in Rushdie's fiction, and indeed this amorphous world yields Saleem 'both less and more ... than he had expected'. Time falls away ('hours or days or weeks'), scale becomes distorted ('the jungle was gaining in size'), they surrender to 'the logic of the jungle ... the insanity of the jungle ... the turbid, miasmic state of mind which the jungle induced' (*MC* 350–1). The difference of texture has to do with the depth of reference in the passage. We are made to think not so much of Swift's disoriented Gulliver as of Conrad's Marlow from *Heart of Darkness* ('Going up that river was like travelling back to the earliest beginnings of the world...'); perhaps of the characters in J. G. Ballard's *The Drowned World*, driven back in their dreams to an archaic, antediluvian existence.[20] The soldiers' project, 'which had begun far away in the real world', has acquired 'in the altered light of the Sundarbans a quality of absurd fantasy which enabled them to dismiss it once and for all'. History has not forgotten them, in that they are haunted by the ghosts of those they have killed ('each night [the forest] sent them new punishments'). And when they have done penance enough, they begin to regress towards infancy, before being brought again to themselves: 'so it seemed that the magic jungle, having tormented them with their misdeeds, was leading them by the hand towards a new adulthood' (*MC* 351–3).

Saleem, however, has to undergo a more complex process of renewal, involving not only rebirth but 'reconception'; and it is here that we have the last twist of the metaphor. 'But finally the forest found a way through to him; one afternoon, when rain pounded down on the trees and boiled off them as steam, Ayooba Shaheed Farooq saw the buddha sitting under his tree while a blind, translucent serpent bit, and poured venom into, his heel' (*MC* 353). Whereas Sterne's *Tristram Shandy* begins with the actual conception of Tristram, *Midnight's Children* appears not to include this detail (we focus exclusively on his birth). But what Rushdie has actually done, it seems, is to 'delay' Saleem's real conception until this moment later in his life. The blind snakes of the Sundarbans are as it were spermatozoa; the bite in the heel (mythologically a vulnerable part) is the decisive moment where life takes hold. This provides an unusually complete, elaborated, and satisfying version of the metaphor of rebirth, which imitates 'all the myriad complex processes that go to make a man', linking him to the evolutionary chain of DNA as well as to his own personal history ('I was rejoined to the past...'). But Saleem, though reconceived, is not yet reborn; significantly, he cannot yet remember his birthright, his name. The dislocations of the magical journey continue, as the four move (again like Conrad's Marlow) 'ever further into the dense uncertainty of the jungle' and come upon a 'monumental Hindu temple' appropriately decorated with 'friezes of men and women...coupling in postures of unsurpassable athleticism and...of highly comic absurdity' (*MC* 354–5). The temple is a shrine to the 'fecund and awful' goddess Kali – a reminder that the Sundarbans episode functions first and foremost as an *erotic* fantasy; the descent into hell is also a recovery of our repressed, elemental selves.

The rebirth motifs in this section prepare Saleem for his deliverance from Pakistan in Parvati's basket and his return to India – where, as the narrative hurries self-consciously and precipitously towards its conclusion, the last five chapters feature the rise of Indira Gandhi's Congress Party (with herself as the 'Black Widow', the wicked witch to balance Parvati); the symbolic destruction by Sanjay's troops of the magicians' ghetto, and the persecution and elimination of the children of midnight themselves in the grotesque episode of the vasectomists. This reflects the scandalous abuse of the mass sterilization programme of 1975, a genocidal crime against the Indian people that has had other reverberations in Rushdie's work. The fulfilment of the symmetrical intention of the plot is reached when the unmanned Saleem marries his true midnight sister, Parvati-the-Witch, who is pregnant with Shiva's child: thus ensuring that their son Aadam Sinai – the son to all three of them – is actually the true great-grandchild of the couple who glimpsed each other through the perforated sheet in the first chapter of the novel. Parvati is killed in the ghetto; her sickly child suffers in sympathy with 'the larger, macrocosmic disease', recovering after the emergency thanks to the ministrations of 'a certain washerwoman, Durga by name, who had wet-nursed him through his sickness, giving him the daily benefit of her inexhaustibly colossal breasts' (*MC* 408, 429). Shiva has played his destructive part in the suppression of the midnight children, provoking Saleem even to lie about his death; but, unlike the errors in the narrative (deliberate and unintentional), which stand their dubious ground, this lie is retracted (*MC* 425–7). And so Saleem can move towards his summation with a clear conscience. 'Shiva and Saleem, victor and victim; understand our rivalry, and you will gain an understanding of the age in which you live. (The reverse of this statement is also true.)' (*MC* 416–7). In fact both sets of terms are reversible here, which is presumably Rushdie's intention – reminding us once again of the licence of fiction to equivocate, to have it both ways. It remains only for Saleem to marry the strong-armed Padma, and for Rushdie/Saleem to leave us drowsed with the fume of the pickle factory where the fiction is being confected; surrendering himself, his multiple selves (it seems, willingly enough), to the numbers marching in millions, to the multitudinous identity of the new and always renewable nation. And surrendering his novel, it might be added, to the multiplicity of its possible readings.

4

Shame

Published only two years after *Midnight's Children*, which had enjoyed such extraordinary success, Rushdie's third novel *Shame* brought disappointment. First to the reviewers, who were generally unenthusiastic; then to Rushdie himself, when it failed to win the Booker Prize that year. (The author's public displeasure on this occasion was the beginning of a soured relationship with the 'literary world' – or, at least, its gossip columnists.[1]) Finally, it has to be said that Rushdie's critics have tended to line up against the novel, treating it as the weak twin or dark shadow of *Midnight's Children*. Timothy Brennan finds it 'simply meaner, seedier, a bad joke'; Aijaz Ahmad 'bleak and claustrophobic', deformed by racism and sexism; Catherine Cundy 'a model of closed construction'.[2] Malise Ruthven suggested that 'the whole novel recalls nothing so much as the crude drawings of Steve Bell, the British radical cartoonist'. James Harrison observes that '*Midnight's Children* is a Hindu novel and *Shame* a Muslim one', stressing the continuity but also the essential difference between them; an implicit judgement which is spelt out by Keith Booker, reflecting on 'why Islam so often surfaces in Rushdie's fiction as a symbol of monologic thought. Time and again, Rushdie emphasizes the fact that Islam is the religion of one God, a monotheism that forms a particularly striking symbol in the context of heteroglossic, polytheistic India.'[3] Rushdie has protested that this is a misreading ('it's...wrong to see *Midnight's Children* as the India book and *Shame* as the Pakistan book'), but the conclusion is hard to resist – especially when in the same interview quoted here he refers to the two novels in comparative terms: *Shame* is, he concedes, 'nastier than *Midnight's Children*, or at least the nastiness goes on in a more sustained way...it's not written so affectionately...it's a harder and darker book.'[4]

As has been suggested in Chapter 1, one of the recurrent problems in *Shame* is the instability of its fictional discourse, which in turn has something to do with the instability of Pakistan itself and Rushdie's own ambivalent feelings towards it. What kind of book is this, about what kind of place, and inhabited by what kind of characters? These questions cannot be avoided because Rushdie raises them within the text, in a series of anecdotes which are relevant to the subject and genesis of the novel. The most important of these concerns the creation of Pakistan itself, the political entity and the name.

> It is well known that the term 'Pakistan', an acronym, was originally thought up in England by a group of Muslim intellectuals. P for the Punjabis, A for the Afghans, K for the Kashmiris, S for Sind and the 'tan', they say, for Baluchistan....A palimpsest obscures what lies beneath. To build Pakistan it was necessary to cover up Indian history, to deny that Indian centuries lay just beneath the surface of Pakistani Standard Time. (*S.* 87)

Unlike the creation of modern India, endorsed in all its miscellaneousness in *Midnight's Children*, the creation of Pakistan is presented as an unnatural birth, 'a duel between two layers of time, the obscured world forcing its way back through what-had-been-imposed'. The palimpsest peels and fragments; perhaps, Rushdie concludes, 'the place was just *insufficiently imagined* ... a miracle that went wrong'. The critical temptation is to respond that Rushdie's novel of Pakistan is contaminated with the same failure of imagination: the layers of discourse peel, the fiction fails to cohere.

It may be thought disconcerting, for example, that the Rushdie who understands 'the importance of escaping from autobiography'[5] should wander into the text in carpet slippers to tell us how he 'returned home, to visit my parents and sisters and to show off my firstborn son' (*S.* 26), and that he should derisively mimic the arguments of those native Pakistanis who would deny him a voice: '*Poacher! Pirate! We reject your authority. We know you, with your foreign language wrapped around you like a flag: speaking about us in your forked tongue, what can you tell but lies?*' (*S.* 28). These gestures have the effect of undermining Rushdie's attempt to provide an imaginative location for his story. 'The country in this story is not Pakistan, or not quite. There are two countries, real and fictional, occupying the same space, or almost the same space. My story, my fictional country exist, like myself, at a slight angle to reality' (S. 29). Rushdie has legitimately claimed, in an essay, that the only 'frontiers' in fiction are 'neither political nor imaginative but linguistic' (IH 69). It is unnerving, therefore, that he should describe himself at one moment as 'inventing what never happened to me' (S. 28), with all the confidence of fiction, and yet insisting at another that 'I have not made this up' (S. 241). The distinction becomes precarious when Rushdie switches to the discourse of the 'realistic novel', inserting a two-page dossier of 'real-life material' from contemporary Pakistan (which includes details of a contested mark in 'my youngest sister's geography essay'), alongside incriminating evidence relating to state censorship, industrial production, Ayub Khan's alleged Swiss bank account, and the execution of Zulfikar Ali Bhutto – whose fictional stand-in, Iskander Harappa, awaits the same fate later in the novel. Rushdie assures us at this point that he prefers the form of what he disingenuously calls his 'modern fairy-tale' because realism 'can break a writer's heart' (S. 69–70); but this kind of prevarication can try a reader's patience. On the same terms, one might also question the strategy of citing within the text a tragic anecdote from London (concerning a Pakistani father who killed his daughter for a sexual transgression) as the basis for his central character: 'Sufiya Zenobia grew out of the corpse of that murdered girl.' Rushdie readily confides to us the story of his story:

> All stories are haunted by the ghosts of the stories they might have been. Anna Muhammad haunts this book; I'll never write about her now. And other phantoms are here as well, earlier and now ectoplasmic images connecting shame and violence. These ghosts, like Anna, inhabit a country that is entirely unghostly: no spectral 'Peccavistan', but Proper London. (S. 116–17)

And predictably enough, two other instances from 'Proper London' follow – instances that might (as in a way they do) find their way more appropriately into The Satanic Verses. In the later novel, these fictional frames and postmodern juxtapositioning serve a larger and wonderfully realized aesthetic purpose. But the trouble with these passages (and others like them) in Shame is that the ribs of Rushdie's intention show too uncomfortably through the structure. Some critics have tried to defend these discordant elements with the argument that Rushdie is making a deliberate experiment in *Shame* with the 'new journalism' in the genre of the non-fiction novel;[6] but the elements themselves remain too oddly assorted, miscellaneous, for the reader to be quite convinced.

The uncertainty of tone identifiable here is reflected in the handling of the central narrative, concerning the rivalry of two dynastic families. Whereas *Midnight's Children* had come to life with the discovery of Saleem's first-person voice, Rushdie retreats to the third person in *Shame*. And he distances himself still further from the story he has to tell with the framing device of an observer (or voyeur) through whose perspective, and as it were involuntary participation, we gain access to the narrative. This is Omar Khayyam Shakil, the 'peripheral' hero of the novel, whom we meet in the first of the novel's five sections, entitled 'Escapes from the Mother Country' – a phrase which relevantly runs together allusions to both birth and exile. In his role as marginal man, voyeur, 'living at the edge of the world', Omar is in some sense a surrogate for Rushdie as author (who has been described by Homi Bhabha as a writer 'living at the edge of the Enlightenment'[7]); 'at least he has a vivid imagination', we are told, and he reads all the right books (*S*. 32–3). But Omar is fully realized as an independent and autonomous character, passive though he may be, and convincingly projected into the role of the recognizable Rushdie hero from the bizarre circumstances of his birth and upbringing. He is the child of three mothers, the formidable Shakil sisters, whose grasping father has died on the first page of the novel leaving them in doubtful control of their decaying fortunes. The shared pregnancy occurs after a scandalous party, leaving the identity of his mother as well as his father a mystery. (Rushdie resists allegorical readings, but, if we were to follow up the Methwold hint from *Midnight's Children*, the father would be the departing Raj and the three mothers India, Pakistan, and Bangladesh.) Omar is left free to wander the ramshackle Shakil mansion, Nishapur, itself a metaphor of postcolonial Pakistan; it is here that he acquaints himself with the long history of his birthplace, acquiring the essential, identifying information that Aadam Aziz had gained in the earlier novel from Tai the boatman: 'he explored beyond history into what seemed the positively archaeological antiquity of "Nishapur".... On one occasion he lost his way completely and ran wildly about like a time-traveller who has lost his magic capsule and fears he will never emerge from the disintegrating history of his race' (S. 31). There are traces here, too, of Flapping Eagle's radical disorientation in *Grimus*.

But Omar's main role is as vantage point, voyeur: as he confesses to himself at the end, during a dream of interrogation in the police cells, 'I am a peripheral man.... Other persons have been the principal actors in my life-story; Hyder and Harappa, my leading men. Immigrant and native, Godly and profane, military and civilian. And several leading ladies. I watched from the wings, not knowing how to act' (S. 283). For a moment he sounds almost like Jane Austen's Fanny Price paralysed at Mansfield Park ('I cannot act'[8]), the victim of others' plots and her own diminished affectivity; and indeed this is his role, exercising no volition of his own but providing the moral dimension of other characters' experience.

The novel really begins (or begins again) with the second section, 'The Duellists', and the formal announcement in the first paragraph here (which reads like the exordium of an eighteenth-century novel) of key elements in the plot.

> This is a novel about Sufiya Zinobia, elder daughter of Raza Hyder and his wife Bilquis, about what happened between her father and Chairman Iskander Harappa, formerly Prime Minister, now defunct, and about her surprising marriage to a certain Omar Khayyam Shakil, physician, fat man, and for a time the intimate crony of that same Isky Harappa...(S. 59)

The note of detachment, ironic demonstration, could not be more decisively sounded; and Rushdie is prepared to discharge the traditional responsibilities of dynastic fiction. We need a family tree (and the interlaced family tree is duly provided at the beginning of the novel). We have to be introduced to Sufiya's mother, Bilquis, and Bilquis's father, Mahmoud Kemal, who also runs an Empire: 'the Empire Talkies, a fleapit of a picture theatre in the old quarter of the town.' The town is Delhi; this is still India before Independence, and before 'the famous moth-eaten partition that chopped up the old country and handed Al-Lah a few insect-nibbled slices of it' (S. 60–1). But fathers are quickly dispatched in this novel, as we have already observed from the sudden departure of Mr Shakil – part of Rushdie's design being to illustrate the way women are the victims of masculine ambition, lust, fanaticism, cruelty, and incompetence. And so Mahmoud is killed by a bomb that destroys his cinema when he tries to show films that cross the religious divide – 'even going to the pictures had become a political act' (*S.* 61): a bomb that also lights a fuse, anticipating the novel's apocalyptic ending. Bilquis wanders dazed and naked in the streets, providing one of Rushdie's most memorable images of the dislocated and dispossessed:

> O Bilquis. Naked and eyebrowless beneath the golden knight.... All migrants leave their pasts behind, although some try to pack it into bundles and boxes – but on the journey something seeps out of the treasured mementoes and old photographs, until even their owners fail to recognize them, because it is the fate of migrants to be stripped of history, to stand naked amidst the scorn of strangers upon whom they see the rich clothing, the brocades of continuity and the eyebrows of belonging. (*S.* 63–4)

Bilquis is rescued by Raza Hyder, and her marriage introduces her to the dynastic Hyder family, with the bizarre mating rituals and complex social interaction described in chapter 5, 'The Wrong Miracle'; and also to the family stories, 'because the stories, such stories, were the glue that held the clan together, binding the generations in webs of whispered secrets'. It also projects her into the story, 'the juiciest and goriest of all the juicygory sagas', in which like it or not she has to play her part (*S.* 76–7). Bilquis's part is to give birth to Sufiya Zinobia, herself the 'wrong miracle', in that she is a daughter rather than Raza's expected son; and as such she is destined to serve as an image of Pakistan itself, which has been described a few pages earlier as 'the miracle that went wrong' (*S.* 89, 87). Sufiya's birth has been preceded by the symbolic stillbirth of a son, who was strangled by the umbilical cord in the womb; a son whose ghostly unhappened life, jointly fantasized by the parents, ironically suggests an alternative and (who knows) happier history for Pakistan. The stillborn son may also be seen as part of the system of imaginative insufficiency alluded to above: the people of new Pakistan 'had been given a bad shock by independence, by being told to think of themselves, as well as the country itself, as new. Well, their imaginations simply weren't up to the job.'

'History was old and rusted' (*S*. 81–2), and even Raza Hyder is unable to move it.

The narrator of *Midnight's Children* confessed to a weakness for symmetry, that obtrusive patterning of events that is characteristic of the comic vision; and this quality is equally foregrounded in the black comedy of *Shame*. Timothy Brennan draws attention to the no doubt ironic repetition of the mystical number three in the structure: three mothers, three families, three countries, three religions, three capitals.[9] The 'duellists' themselves, Raza and Iskander, are ushered into battle (first, over a woman) on the same page that sees Bilquis and Rani consigned to their parallel fates: 'Meanwhile, two wives are abandoned in their separate exiles, each with a daughter who should have been a son' (*S*. 104). Iskander's wife Rani has given birth to Arjumand, whose fiercely denied femaleness will earn her the nickname 'the Virgin Ironpants'. (As we shall see, Rani's other function is to weave her allegorical shawls.) Meanwhile, Sufiya has been stricken with a brain disease that dislocates her time sense, further underlining her association with a Pakistan progressively unable (or unwilling) to take its place in history.

> Two months after Raza Hyder departed into the wilderness to do battle with the gas-field dacoits, his only child Sufiya Zinobia contracted a case of brain fever that turned her into an idiot.... Despairing of military and civilian doctors [Bilquis] turned to a local Hakim who prepared an expensive liquid distilled from cactus roots, ivory dust and parrot feathers, which saved the girl's life but which (as the medicine man had warned) had the effect of slowing her down for the rest of her years, because the side-effect of a potion so filled with the elements of longevity was to retard the progress of time inside the body of anyone to whom it was given. (*S*. 100)

Dislocation from historical time features in all Rushdie's fictions, from *Grimus* to *The Moor's Last Sigh*, and in each case it is a curse, an unwelcome distinction that deprives the afflicted person of the possibility of interacting with others. Here, as later in *The Satanic Verses*, it also symbolizes the ideological war on history, on (Western) time, conducted by militarized Islamic absolutism, invoking for its own purposes the incontrovertible and claustrophobic simultaneity of the Koran.

In section III ('Shame, Good News and the Virgin') the duellists are brought closer to the crisis of their confrontation.

Isky Harappa abandons the hedonistic life he has shared with Omar Shakil and takes a new mistress, history, as part of a 'process of remaking himself' that leads to his becoming Prime Minister (S. 125, 172); while Raza Hyder frets in his shadow, conscious of Harappa's greater political astuteness. But, if the comic perspective Rushdie imposes on his materials requires symmetry, symmetry also requires weddings, and the families are further (dis)united by the failure of the proposed alliance between Isky's nephew Haroun Harappa and Ryder's younger daughter Naveed – who ditches Haroun in preference for a polo-playing policeman the day before the ceremony; which is nevertheless carried out, to everyone's consternation, with the substitute groom. This passage (S. 162–72) is one of the comic triumphs of the novel; including the shocking scene where Sufiya, overcome by shame, a 'pouring-in to her too-sensitive spirit of the great abundance of shame in that tormented tent', physically attacks her sister's new husband, burying her teeth in his neck. Ryder's unexpected son-in-law Tulvar Ulhaq does turn out to have his uses, however, as his magic-realist clairvoyancy enables him to detect crimes even before they are committed. Meanwhile the disreputable but indispensable hero Omar has also 'fallen for his destiny' by marrying the afflicted daughter Sufiya, whom he has treated in his profession as a doctor during one of her seizures. These take the form of her succumbing (as at her sister's wedding) to a 'plague of shame', and it is her embodiment of the moral theme of the novel, the scarcely translatable *sharam,* that identifies her as a secular saint. It is this role that provides the mysterious centre of the novel, her encounter with evil that leaves the limiting paradigms of the 'new journalism' behind. 'What is a saint?' the novel asks us, proposing the answer: 'A saint is a person who suffers in our stead' (S. 141). And even the bemused Raza perceives 'a kind of symmetry here' (S. 161).

The third section concludes with a summary of the action so far. 'Once upon a time there were two families, their destinies inseparable even by death' (S. 173); the note of tragic fate is deliberately sounded. But, as is often the case in drama – in Greek drama, and in Shakespeare – despite the men's fantastic political tricks before high heaven it is the female roles that somehow come to typify this fate. Here, the recurring contrast between the two Hyder sisters Sufiya and Naveed ('What contrasts in these girls!' (*S.* 137)) and the two sequestered wives Bilquis Hyder and Rani Harappa assumes greater significance. As Rushdie observes:

> I had thought, before I began, that what I had on my hands was an almost excessively masculine tale, a saga of sexual rivalry, ambition, power, patronage, betrayal, death, revenge. But the women seem to have taken over; they marched in from the peripheries of the story to demand the inclusion of their own tragedies, histories, and comedies, obliging me to couch my narrative in all manner of sinuous complexities, to see my 'male' plot refracted, so to speak, through the prisms of its reverse and 'female' side. It occurs to me that the women knew precisely what they were up to – that their stories explain, and even subsume, the men's. (*S.* 173)

Not only is this the clearest insight into Rushdie's handling of gender politics in the novel;[10] the comment is significant, also, as it reflects on Rushdie's conscious deployment of different genres. Does one not catch an echo, in this parodic formal categorizing, of Polonius' pedantic recommendation of the players in *Hamlet*? If so, it is entirely appropriate, given the theatrical denouement that is in preparation, with its references to this play.

The fourth and longest section of *Shame* ('In the Fifteenth Century', with allusion to the Hegiran calendar) takes us further into the fantastic politics of this fantasy Pakistan. And each of its four chapters is fantastic in a different way. The first (ironically titled 'Alexander the Great') provides a deliberately de-synchronized history of Isky Harappa's years in power, partly through low-voltage gossip and media refraction but mainly through the highly charged and contradictory recollections of his daughter, Arjumand, and his wife Rani – which show that 'no two sets of memories ever match, even when their subject is the same' (*S.* 191). Arjumand's self-imposed function is to sanctify her father's memory, 'to transmute the preserved fragments of the past into the gold of myth' (*S.* 181). But Rani assumes a more sibylline role. Her eighteen embroidered shawls are a central metaphor in the novel (and anticipate, incidentally, the analogous device of Aurora Zogoiby's paintings in *The Moor's Last Sigh*). Not only do they provide, in four pages (*S.* 191–5), a terrifying, telescoped account of corruption and cruelty, an object lesson in the perversions of power; they also remind us that it is the female vision that has understood and registered this. The badminton shawl, the slapping shawl, the kicking shawl, the hissing shawl; 'in silver thread she revealed the arachnid terror of those days'. The torture shawl, the obliterating white shawl, the swearing shawl; the shawls of international shame and the election shawls, culminating in the 'carnage' of the seventeenth shawl, the shawl of hell, and the final unsparing shawl depicting the murder of Little Mir Harappa: 'she had delineated his body with an accuracy that stopped the heart.' It is not only (as the narrator concedes) that women have taken over the plot; the moral and imaginative vision of *Shame* is articulated from a female standpoint. This is another reason, perhaps, why the awkward formal gestures referred to earlier seem so inappropriate.

The second chapter returns to Sufiya Zinobia, and her operations as 'one of those supernatural beings, those exterminating or avenging angels, or werewolves, or vampires, about whom we are happy to read in stories' (*S.* 197). The inventory of styles is more productive than the abstract gesticulations of form. Rushdie has confirmed that Stevenson's paradigmatic Dr Jekyll and Mr Hyde lie behind the complementary conceptions of the doctor Omar Shakil and Raza Hyder; but the beast Hyde also inhabits the retarded Sufiya, as an image both of her saintly scapegoat 'shame' and also the correlative sexual violence in which it issues. Like other writers who have meditated on the consequences in daily life of the brutal events and revolutions of our times (one thinks of the poetry of Tony Harrison, who wrote *The Blasphemers' Banquet* in solidarity with Rushdie in 1989), Rushdie has made it clear that he sees an intimate connection between public life and sexual behaviour – especially in the context of *Shame*: 'the book is set in Pakistan and it deals, centrally, with the way in which the sexual repressions of that country are connected to the political repressions.'[11] There is an excellent, moving passage in this chapter that presents the uncomprehending consciousness of an innocent:

> There is a thing called the world that makes a hollow noise when you knock your knuckles on it or sometimes it's flat and divided up in books. She knows it is really a picture of a much bigger place called everywhere but it isn't a good picture because she can't see herself in

it, even with a magnifying glass. She puts a much better world into her head, she can see everyone she wants to there. . . .There is a thing that women do at night with their husbands. She does not do it, Shahbanou does it for her. *I hate fish.* . . . But she *is a wife.* She *has a husband.* She can't work this out. The horrible thing and the horrible not-doing-the-thing. She squeezes her eyelids shut with her fingers and makes the babies play. There is no ocean but there is a feeling of sinking. It makes her sick. There is an ocean. She feels its tide. And, somewhere in its depths, a Beast, stirring. (*S.* 213–5)

The use of a restricted consciousness for the paradoxical purpose of clarification is a strategy often used by the post-colonial writer, a technique of altered perspective and estrangement that looks back to Swift. The passage quoted establishes Sufiya in this role, in that what she cannot work out forces us to reflect and reconsider our own assumptions about the domestication of the beast. It is followed shortly afterwards by a chilling account of the sexual murders of four young men, for which the possessed Sufiya is responsible: 'the Beast bursting forth to wreak its havoc on the world' (*S.* 219). She too is the reversible victor/victim: as it were, the lust-crazed Yahoo girl from *Gulliver's Travels* as well as the flayed woman from the 'Digression on Madness' in *A Tale of a Tub.*[12] As the receptacle of their shame, Sufiya becomes also 'the collective fantasy of a stifled people, a dream born of their rage' (*S.* 263); she too carries her dead brother within her, and the lost hope he represented.

But the preordained plot of history drives the male plot of the novel, and the chapter on the fall of Harappa at Hyder's hands returns us to the problem of the fictional discourse in *Shame,* discussed above. On the one hand, we have the powerful image of Iskander in the death cell, 'death's baby', with the noose tightening around his neck a clear reference back to his strangled son: '*Yes, I am being unmade*' (*S.* 231). It is the full reversal of the birth motif in *Midnight's Children*; and here the fiction maintains its own imaginative parabola. But then Rushdie grasps again at the handrails of history in order to 'verify' his story. Of the trial of Harappa we are told: 'All this is on the record', 'All this is well known'; baldly, even the proverbial 'facts are facts' (*S.* 228, 231, 233). Even if it could be argued that the last of these asseverations is ironic, it certainly confuses the reader to have different criteria of 'truth' applied as it were simultaneously – as if Rushdie were somehow reinsuring his fiction with documentary evidence. There is a danger of our finding ourselves in that dubious fictional space where, as Henry James remarked, details have ceased to be things of fact and yet not become things of truth.[13] This fatal hesitation also affects the last chapter of section IV ('Stability'), which follows the establishment of Hyder's fundamentalist power. It begins with a two-page discussion of a performance in London of Buchner's play *Danton's Death*, and the implications of the drama for Pakistani politics (S. 240–2). Then there is a distinctly awkward intervention on the new fundamentalism, which is introduced with an apology ('May I interpose a few words here on the subject of the Islamic revival? It won't take long'), and then pursued in an uncompromisingly journalistic manner: 'So-called Islamic "fundamentalism" does not spring, in Pakistan, from the people. It is imposed on them from above' (S. 250–1). Such lapses of judgement recall Timothy Brennan's not unreasonable comment, that Rushdie's journalism lacks the 'bipartisan' dimension of his fiction;[14] furthermore, the two categories certainly seem to trip over each other here. Alternative fictions may happily coexist, but competing truth claims tend to cancel each other out.

Within this chapter, nevertheless, the novel is concentrating its imaginative energies in preparation for the fifth and last section 'Judgment Day' – which, significantly, allows no authorial intervention to diffuse the gathering conviction of its climax. Omar has a vision of the 'two selves' of his wife, Sufiya, a familiar Rushdie trope, and begins to recognize (and to fear) the 'smouldering fire of the Beast' which he recognizes in her (S. 235). When she escapes the confinement of her husband and father to begin a reign of terror as the white panther, Omar asks himself whether 'human beings are capable of discovering their nobility in their savagery' (S. 254), and the ghost of Iskander suggests to him that his daughter has become a natural force, like a river in flood, that will destroy our human constructions, whether physical or imaginative: 'everything yields to its fury...no dykes or barriers have been made to hold her' (S. 256). It is not surprising that Rushdie has confessed that he became afraid of his own creation in Sufiya; what she meant, how she fitted into the accelerating vision of 'the nature of evil'.[15]

The last section is played out at this high pitch: back where the novel began, at Nishapur on the altar of the high hills of the city of Q, and in sight of the Impossible Mountains. (Responsiveness to the moral geography of the subcontinent was something Rushdie learnt from Kipling, and the last stages of the journey of Kim and his lama are surely not forgotten here.) Judgement is to fall on Raza Hyder, brought to their house by Omar to be impaled on the blades of the Shakil sisters' lethal contraption, constructed in earlier years – the curiously apposite 'dumb waiter' that works like an Iron Maiden. Raza's wife, Bilquis, dies of a fever, and eventually Omar gives himself up, a willing sacrifice, to the retributive fury of the Beast. But before this apotheosis it is he who must conduct the epilogue, as he featured in the prologue to the novel. It is he who negotiates the dizzying levels of reality that press in at the end, within the old house that is alternately shrinking and expanding, unsure in his own fever 'whether things were happening or not' (S. 273–5); there are shades of the Sundarbans here. It is he who is given access to a vision of the future (as at the end of each cycle of Shakespeare's history plays), 'of what would happen after the end ... arrests, retribution, trials, hangings, blood, a new cycle of shamelessness and shame' (S. 276–7). And it is Omar who finally understands and interiorizes this shame, sharing in full consciousness the symbolic possession of his wife. 'The Beast has many faces. It can take any shape it chooses. He felt it crawl into his belly and begin to feed' (S. 279). Omar becomes, one might even suggest, a kind of Hamlet, 'crawling between heaven and earth', consumed by the end with self-disgust at what is rotten in the state of Peccavistan. This suggestion is reinforced by Omar's sense of the 'gaping mouth of the void', of the 'supernatural frontier' he is approaching (S. 268), and also by his mothers' retelling of a shameful family secret, 'the worst tale in history', involving a fratricidal sexual betrayal: 'this is a family in which brothers have done the worst of things to brothers'. In Chunni's perverse taunt to Omar, concerning his paternity, we can even hear a clear echo of Hamlet's reproach to his mother. Omar is told, 'Your brother's father was an archangel....But you, your maker was a devil out of hell' (S. 277–8).

On first arriving back at Nishapur Omar perceived that his mothers had set up what is described as a 'demented theatre' for the novel's last scene, and so these dramatic parallels are perhaps authorized – continuing a pattern of Shakespearian intertext that becomes a more pronounced feature in Rushdie's later novels. The three sisters themselves, called hags and witches by Raza, are clearly kin to the Weird Sisters, as Raza himself is a version of the usurping Macbeth. But the last scene belongs emphatically to fiction, where 'all the stories ha[ve] to end together', since 'the power of the Beast of shame cannot be held for long within any one frame of flesh and blood'. And the stories do end together, after Omar has surrendered to the terrible, murderous embrace of his inspired wife, in an explosion that begins in the house, starting a fireball 'rolling outwards to the horizon like the sea', becoming a silent cloud, a cloud 'in the shape of a giant, grey, and headless man' (S. 286): a cloud much like the apocalyptic nuclear cloud that casts its shadow more than once in Rushdie's novels. The rest was silence, for the next five years at least, while Rushdie was working on his own explosive device: *The Satanic Verses*.

5

The Satanic Verses

The Satanic Verses is a novel bristling with difficulty. This is due not so much to the cloud of controversy that has settled over it, as to the complexity of the novel itself, which makes the most disinterested reading a challenge. This complexity is no mere provocative, postmodernist 'top dressing' but arises from the nature and intensity of the metaphysical speculation that lies at the heart of the work. There is a dense, nuclear fusion of ideas, grouped around the nature of modern identity, personal and national/ethnic; the relationship between our instinct for good and evil; the implications of this for our understanding of human disposition and potentialities; the nature of the 'reality' within which we are required to live out our lives. These ideas are galvanized by what may even be described as a dangerous experiment with the limits of imagination, which involves testing to destruction the coherences we ordinarily rely upon, via discontinuity, dream, fantasy, and psychosis; and exploring – by living through it – the nature and authority of 'inspiration', including religious revelation. But let us remember, as Rushdie himself and some of his more perceptive critics have reminded us, that despite the seriousness of these preoccupations, we are dealing with a novel – even, a comic novel – which, while it engages with other ideological discourses, does so (or at least attempts to do so) on its own terms. Rushdie presented his own formal defence in the essay 'In Good Faith' (1990: *IH* 393–414), and the position outlined here has been supported by many other novelists and critics.[1]

One of the difficulties has to do with the extreme formal complexity generated by Rushdie's fictional scheme. As he conceded in a newspaper interview that coincided with the publication of the novel in September 1988:

The Satanic Verses is very big. There are certain kinds of architecture that are dispensed with. *Midnight's Children* had history as a scaffolding on which to hang the book; this one doesn't. And since it's so much about transformation I wanted to write it in such a way that the book itself was metamorphosing all the time. Obviously the danger is that the book falls apart.[2]

Well: the book has 'fallen apart' in one sense, or been torn apart, dismembered by faction and misrepresentation, from which it can hardly recover. But Rushdie put his 'big' novel together with ingenuity as well as creative energy. The structure and the writing of the *Verses* are as intricate as the conception is complex, and we should begin by trying to describe how the fiction is used to articulate and illuminate the governing ideas. Engaging at the most summary level, we could say that the novel is about two friends, their intense, often antagonistic relationship with each other, with their sexual partners, and with the society around them – which is subjected to radical criticism. In the end, one of them commits suicide, while the other survives with a degree of salvaged optimism and a new perspective on love. This description as it happens also fits Lawrence's *Women in Love* – a novel to which *The Satanic Verses* does indeed have intriguing resemblances, not least in the nature of the disintegration against which the characters are forced to struggle in order to survive, and the disconcerting 'doubleness' and reversibility of the discourse. But this comparison also highlights the uniqueness of Rushdie's novel, which, however many allusions, references, and parallels may be found within it, cannot be reduced to the sum of its influences. No more than can Joyce's *Ulysses*. These influences include, it must be said, the Bible and the Koran, the Indian epics, Sufi texts, Virgil, Dante, Shakespeare, Blake, Dickens, Bulgakov, Beckett – and of course Joyce himself. Not to mention the cinematic tradition of three continents, and a representative swathe of contemporary (that is to say, 1980s) British, Indian, and other cultures. One needs to 'home in' on the specificity of Rushdie's text, and the specific strategies and solutions he has employed to deliver it.

The two friends, Gibreel Farishta and Saladin Chamcha, are (specifically) Indians; more specifically, they are living (most of the time) in modern Britain; more specifically still, they are media people (one in film, one in radio); and most specifically of all, they have arrived in Britain as the miraculous survivors of an Air India jet bombed by terrorists high over London. We are introduced to them, on the first page, literally 'flying' to earth. This is not realist discourse – though what are later called 'the polluted waters of the real' (*SV* 309) flow freely enough through the novel. As in Auden's poem 'Musée des Beaux Arts', we have seen 'something amazing, a boy falling out of the sky'; and the fiction that follows will more than maintain that extraordinary trajectory. What happens is that the two 'fall' not only literally into a decaying Britain but also by the novelist's sleight of hand into each other; and with the help of his well-practised time-travelling gifts into several parallel narratives: unravelling in contemporary London, seventh-century Arabia, twentieth-century Pakistan; diversified with excursions to Buenos Aires and Bombay, memories of the voyages of Vasco da Gama, the execution of Charles I, and the Battle of Hastings. We learn through flashback of the film career of Gibreel Farishta (cinema itself serving again as the modern metamorphic form *par excellence*), and the loss of faith that brings 'a terrible isolation' upon him; the tragic end of one affair (in the death of Rekha Merchant) and the beginning of another (with a symbolic woman mountaineer named Alleluia Cone). Simultaneously – and simultaneity is one of the novel's jewelled levers – we are told of the English education and marriage of Saladin Chamcha, and his success as a radio 'voice': 'he ruled the airwaves of Britain' (*SV* 60). All this helps him to achieve his denial of Bombay, represented by his ageing father and his one-time mistress Zeeny Vakil – who speaks up, appositely enough, in protest at such perverse 'purity', for 'the eclectic, hybridized nature of the Indian artistic tradition' (*SV* 70).

But, since section II delivers the unsuspecting reader along with Gibreel himself into the Arabian desert in the seventh century, we need at this point to address the structure of the novel, in its nine sections, and Gibreel's role as 'time traveller' (and something more) between them. It has been observed[3] that this novel about disintegration and reintegration is itself divided via its odd-and-even-numbered sections. The first four of the 'odd' sections, I to VII (which take up much the longer part, some 400 of the novel's 547 pages), take place in London, while the last, IX, is set in Bombay. The four 'even' sections (each,

73

curiously, 38 pages) contain the magical or dream material. Section II ('Mahound') tells the story of the original revelation to the prophet (including the notorious episode of the 'satanic verses' themselves); section IV, ('Ayesha') begins with a brief encounter with a sinister Imam who resembles Khomeini in exile, before moving on to the story of the girl Ayesha, who lives on butterflies and proposes a pilgrimage from Pakistan to Mecca (simply walking into the sea); section Vl ('Return to Jahilia') relates the story of the establishment of Islam itself, and the power-broking that goes on in the interests of the 'Idea'; while section VIII, ('The Parting of the Arabian Sea') recapitulates the outcome of Ayesha's pilgrimage. The key structural (and psychological) feature is that it is Gibreel, as archangel – specifically, angel of the recitation, he who dictates the word of God to the prophet – who 'dreams' the other, magical narratives. And the handling of the interface between the 'two' texts, two levels of reality, is the supreme test of Rushdie's skill as a narrator.

These 'serial dreams' begin when Gibreel and Saladin are held hostage in the hijacked aircraft (for a symmetrical 111 days), 'marooned on a shining runway around which there crashed the quiet sand-waves of the desert' (*SV* 77).

> Gibreel was sweating from fear: '...every time I go to sleep the dream starts up from where it stopped. Same dream in the same place. As if somebody just paused the video while I went out of the room. Or, or. As if he's the guy who's awake and this is the bloody nightmare. His bloody dream: us. Here. All of it.' (*SV* 83)

As if to confirm that reading can be dangerous, these dreams begin after Gibreel has been reading a creationist pamphlet given to him by a crank about 'a supreme entity controlling all creation' (*SV* 81–2). The strategy of the dream is revealed where Gibreel dreams the Fall ('Shaitan cast down from the sky'), dreams dreaming: 'Sometimes when he sleeps Gibreel becomes aware, without the dream, of himself sleeping, of himself dreaming his own awareness of his dream' (*SV* 91–2). This is where for him 'panic begins', the fear of insanity, as he is forced to question the ground of his own being; but where for us as readers the fun begins, the intriguing play of levels, the skilful and subtle framing of successive fictions within each other.

But when he has rested he enters a different sort of sleep, a sort of not-sleep, the condition that he calls his *listening*, and he feels a dragging pain in the gut, like something trying to be born, and now Gibreel, who has been hovering-above-looking-down, feels a confusion, *who am I*, in these moments it begins to seem that the archangel is actually *inside the prophet*, I am the dragging in the gut, I am the angel being extruded from the sleeper's navel, I emerge, Gibreel Farishta, while my other self, Mahound, lies *listening*, entranced, I am bound to him, navel by navel, by a shining cord of light, not possible to say which of us is dreaming the other. We flow in both directions along the umbilical cord.   (*SV* 110)

There is a dizzying play of fictional perspectives at work here. If Mahound questions his own identity, referring upwards to Gibreel; and Gibreel questions his identity, referring upwards to the author-God, then where exactly are we? If they cannot tell 'which of us is dreaming the other', then what is the point of origin of Rushdie's fiction? It is not unlike the situation in *Hamlet*, where Hamlet (the character in Shakespeare's play) challenges the authenticity of the sentiments uttered by the actor in the play-within-the play – 'What's Hecuba to him or he to Hecuba,/That he should weep for her?'[4] – when the same argument applies by domino effect to Hamlet himself. Fiction collapses into discourse; into what Beckett has most unremittingly analysed as the migrant voice, migrant in an ultimate sense, that travels with its supply of words through all the categories of culture: human individuals as well as texts, documents as well as institutions. Steven Connor has rightly suggested that 'the question of identity' in *The Satanic Verses* is 'closely implicated with the possibilities of fiction',[5] and this is how the imbrication takes place.

We need to be able to 'ride the thermals' in this novel, to respond appropriately to the currents of discourse, the different registers engaged, the light verbal signals given. And Rushdie is prepared to provide alternative metaphors for this process of creation, exchange, interpretation – metaphors often derived (as in previous novels) from the media. Thus Gibreel's point of view is identified as 'sometimes that of the camera and at other moments, spectator. When he's a camera the pee oh vee is always on the move, he hates static shots ... But as the dream shifts, it's always changing form, he, Gibreel, is no longer a mere spectator but the central player, the star' (*SV* 108). We recall what Rushdie said about the form of the novel 'metamorphosing all the time', and here we see exactly what he means. This makes for demanding reading, but, once the principle of the double narration has been grasped, it does make sense – and actually provides some of the novel's most spectacular imaginative effects. We become accustomed to being in two places at once; thus, when in section III Gibreel is held spellbound by Rosa Diamond's stories, we are explicitly reminded of his inextricable involvement with the prophet Mahound (*SV* 150); when in section V he endures a week's tormented sleep in Allie Cone's flat, muttering '*Jahilia, Al-Lat, Hind*', and later sleeptalks in Arabic (*SV* 301, 340), he is understood to be labouring at the articulation of the new religion, the new Idea. When in section VII Gibreel recites the names of the teenage prostitutes at King's Cross, the names are the same as those of the prophet's wives, usurped by the prostitutes in Jahilia (*SV* 460, 382); and when at the end of this chapter Gibreel calls out the name 'Mishal', it is not the distraught Mishal from the Shaandaar Café he is addressing but Mirza's wife Mishal, from the Ayesha story, who is about to be drowned beneath the waters of the Red Sea (*SV* 469, 503). There is even a remarkable paragraph, in the same section [VII], where Gibreel is identified as passing through no fewer than five narratives simultaneously:

> he understands now something of what omnipresence must be like, because he is moving through several stories at once, there is a Gibreel who mourns his betrayal by Alleluia Cone, and a Gibreel hovering over the death-bed of a Prophet, and a Gibreel watching in secret over the progress of a pilgrimage to the sea, waiting for the moment at which he will reveal himself, and a Gibreel who feels, more powerfully every day, the will of the adversary, drawing him ever closer, leading him towards their final embrace: the subtle, deceiving adversary, who has taken the face of his friend, of Saladin his truest friend, in order to lull him into lowering his guard. And there is a Gibreel who walks down the streets of London, trying to understand the will of God. (*SV* 457)

This is a triumph of narrative art, and one that even goes a trick or two, in the treatment of narrative time, beyond Sterne.[6] But the novel is not simply a postmodern puzzle for the reader to solve, although there are enough clues to keep the curious reader happy: in the numerological references (666 the Number of the Beast, 420 a section in the Indian criminal code), and reversible dates such as 1961 that read the same upside down – as (apparently) turning a watch upside down in Bombay will give you the time in London. Then there are the self-descriptive names (Alleluia Cone, Jumpy Joshi) and indeed the whole system of doubled names (Hind/Hind, Mishal/Mishal), that link the levels of the plot; and indicate an indebtedness to both Joyce and Freud.[7]

We may now return from the structure to consider the line of the narrative itself (what is actually witnessed and recorded by this flexible point of view); and then on, as it were out at the other side, to reconsider Rushdie's articulation of his themes. As will have become clear by now, it is no simple matter to do even this, since the 'waking' narrative of the odd-numbered chapters likewise has its fissures and gaps, its equivocations and aporias. Not only does Gibreel live between two worlds, fearing the 'leakage' of one into the other, but Saladin also inhabits an unstable universe, by contagion – both as the satanic half of Gibreel's angel ('the two men, Gibreelsaladin Farishtachamcha, condemned to their endless but also ending angeldevilish fall' (*SV* 5)), forced to share and replicate some of Gibreel's dreams and visions – and also – in his 'own' person – as the metamorphosed victim of a racist society. Section III has delivered the reborn pair into the care of Rosa Diamond, a mysterious woman with a memory as archaic as that of Tai the boatman,[8] and an equally seductive gift for magic-realist narrative. (Critics who have objected to this passage as self-indulgent or superfluous seem not to appreciate its importance in establishing the protocol of the 'hinged' narrative, the jewelled lever of simultaneity referred to earlier.) But only Gibreel is exposed to this, Rosa's stories 'winding round him like a web' (*SV* 146), since Chamcha has meanwhile been arrested by the police as an illegal immigrant – Gibreel's evasion of this treatment, partly because of the appearance of a halo which confounds the law, making him a 'traitor' in Chamcha's eyes. The supernatural level of the narrative reasserts itself as Chamcha gradually turns into a goat, complete with horns, hooves, and tail. The allusion to Lucian's metamorphic *Golden Ass* (its author later identified as colonial subject of an earlier empire (*SV* 243)), foregrounds the real, social significance of this transformation: 'they have the power of description' (explains a friendly manticore), 'and we succumb to the pictures they construct' (*SV* 168). And it is in this disadvantaged condition that Saladin sees 'his' Britain with new eyes: including his wife, Pamela, who, believing him dead, has started an affair with his old friend Jumpy Joshi. She dreams of him confiding in her his new vision of terminal decline: ' "Things are ending," he told her. "This civilization; things are closing in on it. It has been quite a culture, brilliant and foul, cannibal and Christian, the glory of the world. We should celebrate it while we can; until night falls" ' (*SV* 184). Meanwhile Gibreel has also made his way (with his halo) to 'Ellowen Deeowen' London, pursued by 'the fear that God had decided to punish him for his loss of faith by driving him insane', by 'the terror of losing his mind to a paradox, of being unmade by what he no longer believed existed, of turning in his madness into the avatar of a chimerical archangel' (*SV* 189). He is pursued also by the ghost of Rekha Merchant, who transforms 'Proper London' into 'that most protean and chameleon of cities', the underground into a 'subterranean world' out of Virgil or Dante 'in which the laws of time and space had ceased to operate', into a 'hellish maze', a 'labyrinth without a solution' where he must continue his 'epic flight'; and where he is rescued by the reappearance of Allie Cone (*SV* 201).

Section V ('A City Visible but Unseen') is the longest in the novel. It is divided into two chapters, each subdivided into some twenty shorter sections. This episodic structure helps to achieve the effect of dislocation intended here – rather like the 'Wandering Rocks' section in *Ulysses*. The first chapter follows Saladin through Thatcher's Britain. These pages (*SV* 243–94) are the satirical centre of the novel, switching between passages of low realist description and high cultural analysis. The low realism is associated with the Shaandaar Café, where the transformed Chamcha takes refuge, with its improbable proprietor Mr Sufyan, his unforgiving wife Hind (a crossover name), and two teenage daughters, Mishal and Anahita, who are living London to the full. The 'high culture' is represented by Mimi Mamoulian and her playboy friend, Billy Battuta, and the grotesque Hal Valance, whose energetic exploitation of 'adland' draws on Rushdie's own experience of that world. Mimi is well able to defend her jingles against Chamcha's analysis: 'I am an intelligent female. I have read *Finnegans Wake* and am conversant with post-modernist critiques of the West, e.g. that we have here a society capable only of pastiche: a "flattened" world. When I become the voice of a bubble bath, I am entering Flatland knowingly...'. It is Hal who refers to 'Mrs Torture', and understands the kind of newness *she* wants to bring into the world: 'In with the hungry guys with the wrong education. New professors, new painters, the lot. It's a bloody revolution. Newness coming into this country that's stuffed full of fucking old *corpses*' (*SV* 261, 270). The Hot Wax nightclub, with its subversive 'meltdown' ritual of wax effigies, floats somewhere between the two categories as it awaits the fire that will conclude this section; as does Jumpy's jealous critique of Hanif Johnson, right-on lover of the tempting Mishal. 'Hanif was in perfect control of the languages that mattered: sociological, socialistic, black-radical, anti-anti-anti-racist, demagogic, oratorical, sermonic: the vocabularies of power.... But... his envy of Hanif was as much as anything rooted in the other's greater control of the languages of desire.' This makes him painfully aware that 'language is courage: the ability to conceive a thought, to speak it, and by doing so to make it true'. At the same time, Jumpy has a more profound perception which is more to do with language as consciousness than language as power. '*The real language problem: how to bend it shape it, how to let it be our freedom, how to repossess its poisoned wells, how to master the river of words of time of blood: about all that you haven't got a clue*' (*SV* 281). At the end of this chapter, Saladin is returned to human shape, partly 'by the fearsome concentration of his hate' for Gibreel, who now haunts his dreams; as Saladin will symmetrically appear 'on the screen of [Gibreel's] mind' at the end of the next (*SV* 294, 355).

The sixty pages of section V.2 are the most complex and therefore the most tightly organized in the novel. Allie Cone's father provides a prelude, the 'short story' of his life featuring like the interpolated tale in an eighteenth-century novel. Born a Jew in Poland, he has (like Grimus) experienced the extreme horrors of the camps, and denied his past in order to survive: 'he wanted to wipe the slate clean'; ' "l am English now" he would say proudly in his thick East-European accent' (*SV* 297–8). As such he is one of the spokesmen for the discontinuous, disintegrative spirit in the novel. For him, 'this most beautiful and most evil of planets' is beyond redemption, beyond understanding: 'The world is incompatible...Ghosts, Nazis, saints, all alive at the same time; in one spot, blissful happiness, while down the road, the inferno' (*SV* 295). And T. S. Eliot's 'unreal city' from *The Waste Land* is the most visible aspect of this; for him 'the modern city...is the locus classicus of incompatible realities' (*SV* 314). But his philosophy does not save him: 'Otto Cone as a man of seventy-plus jumped into an empty lift-shaft and died' (*SV* 298). (It is possible that Rushdie may have been thinking here of Auschwitz survivor Primo Levi, who committed suicide in 1987.) The rest of the chapter follows Gibreel's own fight against disintegration and the will-to-suicide, alongside an Allie Cone who has had to fight her battles too. She tells Gibreel that she went up the mountain 'to escape good and evil...because that's where all the truth went', deserting the cities where it is 'all made up, a lie'. She is fearful especially of love, 'that archetypal, capitalized djinn', and 'the blurring of the boundaries of the self' (*SV* 314). But Gibreel's jealousy breaks first, blurring other, more catastrophic boundaries: 'the boundaries of the earth broke...and as the spirits of the world of dreams flooded through the breach into the universe of the quotidian, Gibreel Farishta saw God' (*SV* 318).

In the extraordinarily risky, exposed, and comic passage that follows we perceive that the 'God' Gibreel sees is none other than the 'myopic scrivener' Salman Rushdie himself: 'the apparition was balding, seemed to suffer from dandruff and wore glasses.' More vulnerable than the John Fowles who puts in an appearance in his own *The French Lieutenant's Woman*, Rushdie offers himself as a 'hinge' here. It is as if the actor playing Hamlet (to return to the example suggested above) should arraign Shakespeare on stage: who *is* this guy responsible for so much commotion? Why doesn't he leave us in peace? (And indeed the exhausted Gibreel has protested earlier in just such terms: 'If I was God I'd cut the imagination right out of people and then maybe poor bastards like me could get a good night's rest' (*SV* 122).) But the author-God invoked here will not answer the ultimate question: 'Whether We be multiform, plural, representing the union-by-hybridization of such opposites as *Oopar* and *Neechay*, or whether We be pure, stark, extreme, will not be resolved here' (*SV* 319). If God exists, he is the supreme equivocator. Gibreel leaves the relative security of Allie's flat for a renewed assault by a London that has 'grown unstable once again'. There is no defence now from vision ('When you looked through an angel's eyes you saw essences instead of surfaces'), no hiding from the angel's memory of the Fall, no choice in the simple alternative: 'the infernal love of the daughters of men, or the celestial adoration of God' (*SV* 320–1). The comic mode reasserts itself as Blake's prophetic 'map' of London is replaced with the humble A to Z. With this Gibreel sets out to save the city from itself ('the atlas in his pocket was his master plan'), but he finds that 'the city in its corruption refused to submit to the dominion of the cartographers' (*SV* 326–7) – as is proved by his farcical attempt to intervene in a lovers' quarrel at the Angel tube station.

The ghost of Rekha Merchant appears to read Gibreel a lecture on comparative religion. The 'separation of functions, light versus dark, evil versus good, may be straightforward enough in Islam', she observes, but Deuteronomy provides a more archaic and possibly truer formulation: 'I form the light, and create darkness; I make peace and create evil; I the Lord do all these things' (*SV* 323). The fundamental principle of equivocation, reversible values, and significances is never far from the surface. But Gibreel is by this time too far gone in schizophrenia to take heed, and the precise moment of his splitting into two is presented as a cultural phenomenon, via Beckett and Stevenson. 'He had begun to characterize his "possessed", "angel" self as another person: in the Beckettian formula, *Not I. He.* His very own Mr Hyde' (*SV* 340). The media world returns as the stammering film-maker Sisodia proposes that Gabriel should make a comeback in a 'theological', playing none other than the Angel Gibreel – the argument being that if, for once, 'those stories were clearly placed in the artificial, fabricated world of the cinema, it ought to become easier for Gibreel to see them as fantasies, too' (*SV* 347). But Rushdie's design requires that the experiment fails, pre-cipitating Gibreel instead over the edge into psychosis. The sure sign of this is that he sees the split as occurring 'not in him, but in the universe'; there are now 'two realities, this world and another that was also right there, visible but unseen'. This decomposed vision makes everything simple:

No more of these England-induced ambiguities, these Biblical-Satanic confusions!...Forget those son-of-the-morning fictions...How much more straightforward this version was! How much more practical, down-to-earth, comprehensible! – Iblis/Shaitan standing for the darkness, Gibreel for the light. – Out, out with these sentimentalities: *joining, locking together, love.* Seek and destroy: that was all. (*SV* 351–3)

The last of the London sections, 'The Angel Azraeel', brings all these tensions to fulfilment – and provocatively poses the formal problem at the same time. 'What follows is tragedy': or, since tragedy is 'unavailable to modern men and women', at least a 'burlesque for our degraded, imitative times'. But no formal inflection can avoid the underlying question: 'which is, the nature of evil, how it's born, why it grows, how it takes unilateral possession of a many-sided human soul' (*SV* 424). 'It all boiled down to love', reflects Saladin at the beginning, and he tries to implant this principle, celebrating 'the protean, inexhaustible culture of the English-speaking peoples', and even the 'faded splendours' of London itself. 'Resurrection it was then', he concludes, 'roll back that boulder from the cave's dark mouth' (*SV* 397–401). Even overexposure to the 'fast-forward' culture of TV and the scavenging tabloids brings him the image of a grafted tree that reminds him of (and redeems) a tree cut down in anger in his father's garden. But Saladin too is assailed at this point with 'double vision, seeming to look into two worlds at once', when he sees/feels Gibreel bearing down on him, 'the icy shadow of a pair of gigantic wings' (*SV* 416). The media party at Shepperton Studios (a brilliant ten-page set-piece: *SV* 411–21) brings the two into collision. Saladin becomes Iago to Gibreel's Othello, with Allie Cone the innocent victim of his customized 'satanic verses' recited over the telephone; provoking Gibreel to seek vengeance – armed, appropriately enough for this black comedy of communications, with a trumpet rather than a sword.

The crisis of the London plot involves a racially motivated murder enquiry, with a media essay on what the TV camera sees – and (like Lear's 'scurvy politician') does not see, including a police cover up that involves the deaths of both Pamela and Jumpy Joshi and their unborn child. London disintegrates in Gibreel's vision into its destructive elements, its competing cultural descriptions: 'This is no Proper London: not this improper city. Airstrip One, Mahogonny, Alphaville. He wanders through a confusion of languages. Babel... "The gate of God." Babylondon' (*SV* 459). The novel veers at this point (deliberately, confusingly) between the low mimetic of 'derelict kitchen units, deflated bicycle tyres, shards of broken doors, dolls' legs, vegetable refuse', the moralization of these details in 'shattered job prospects, abandoned hopes, lost illusions, expended angers, accumulated bitterness, and a rusting bath', and Blakeian vision, where a 'rotting pile of envy' blossoms into bushes on the concrete, 'needing neither combustible materials nor roots', creating an 'impenetrable... garden of dense intertwined chimeras', like 'the thornwood that sprang up around the palace of the sleeping beauty in another fairy-tale, long ago' (*SV* 461–2). These formal strands are woven together in the burning of the Shaandaar Café, where Gibreel spontaneously rescues Saladin – his evil adversary: 'the fire parting before them like the red sea it has become' (*SV* 468) – the scene also weaving together Rushdie's two fictional worlds, as Ayesha and her pilgrims set out on their journey.

There is less need to comment in detail on the visionary sections, partly because the narrative substance has already been placed within the overall structure and partly because much of the criticism of the novel has focused almost exclusively on this aspect. (Steven Connor has justly remarked that the emphasis on imagined Islam has tended to 'ship the novel safely abroad', away from its intended audience.[9]) But a brief consideration of the principal elements will help to clarify Rushdie's overall design. It is in section II that we are brought closest to the moment of revelation itself (*SV* 112), and the true terror of uncertainty as to the origin of the 'voice'. (Srinivas Aravamudan's essay offers the best commentary on this passage and its implications.[10]) It is here, also, that Mahound is tempted (like Christ in the wilderness) by the 'satanic verses' that would compromise Islam into recognizing the three goddesses Al-Lat, Manat, and Uzza as 'worthy of devotion': verses that he first accepts – in the wake of his uncertainty – and then rejects, partly prompted by Hind, who warns him that 'between Allah and the Three there can be no peace' (*SV* 121). But the unidentified voice has the last unsettling word: '*it was me both times, baba, me first and second also me.* From my mouth, both the statement and the repudiation, verses and converses, universes and reverses, the whole thing, and we all know how my mouth got worked' (*SV* 123).

Or perhaps we do not. The closest we get to interrogating the voice is in section IV, where Gibreel turns on his tormentor/ narrator and tries to ask the fundamental question: where do the words come from? They are 'not his; never his original material. Then whose? Who is whispering in their ears, enabling them to move mountains, halt clocks, diagnose disease? He can't work it out' (*SV* 234). Some critics have argued that we are meant to understand the devil to be the under-narrator of *The Satanic Verses*.[11] And we do need to keep in mind the epigraph Rushdie puts to the novel, taken from Defoe's *History of the Devil*. This presents as it were a *curriculum vitae* for the fallen angel, which at least allows his nomination for the post.

> Satan, being thus confined to a vagabond, wandering, unsettled condition, is without any certain abode; for though he has, in consequence of his angelic nature, a kind of empire in the liquid waste or air, yet this is certainly part of his punishment, that he is ... without any fixed place, or space, allowed him to rest the sole of his foot upon.

There is also, I suggest, in Rushdie's textual self-interrogation, a reference to Hughes's bird-devil from *Crow*, who according to the Manichaean myth refashioned by Hughes takes over the work of creation when God falls asleep; and Crow's vision is God's nightmare, as Gibreel's visions may plausibly be. But it would be false, reductive, to seek to ground a reading of *The Satanic Verses* in exclusively theological terms. The devil we may meet in Rushdie is Blake's devil, or Bulgakov's; and the voice is ultimately Beckett's voice, the furthest we can go in reaching back for the origins of consciousness, the grounding of being in the 'unformulable groping of the mind',[12] the grammatical fiction attached to one pronoun or another. The voice finds a different route in section VI, associated as it is here with the satirist Baal who has parodied the sacred revelation, and who claims (blasphemously but scrupulously), 'I recognize no jurisdiction except that of my Muse; or, to be exact, my dozen Muses' – that is, the twelve favoured prostitutes in the brothel. The reward of his honesty is execution by Mahound: 'Writers and whores. I see no difference here' (*SV* 391–2). Each of the seven scenes or sequences in this section is introduced with the phrase 'Gibreel dreamed...', floating the narrative off into its ambiguous space. And the last is the dream of the death of Mahound himself, to be lamented by Ayesha with her unambiguous faith. 'But Ayesha wiped her eyes, and said: "If there be any here who worshipped the Messenger, let them grieve, for Mahound is dead; but if there be any here who worship God, then let them rejoice, for He is surely alive"' (SV 394). The significance of the 'Untime of the Imam' was briefly considered in Chapter 1. The story of Ayesha dramatizes the clash between philosophies of time, in that her faith and visions stand outside time – as the banyan tree with its half-mile span is a magical space under which her village nestles. She is unmoved by Mirza Saeed's protest that 'this is the modern world' (SV 232), and leads the villagers off on their pilgrimage – including Mirza's wife, Mishal, who has been converted. Section VIII follows the fortunes of the pilgrimage, tacking between two worlds, to the moment when the pilgrims walk into the sea and disappear. We should pay careful attention to the last two pages of this section (SV 505–7) – the sequel to the 'failed' pilgrimage, as the sceptical Mirza, whose wife has been drowned along with the others, comes to terms with his experience. He alone among the survivors claims not to have seen the parting of the Arabian Sea: 'My wife has drowned. Don't come hammering with your questions.' He goes home to Peristan, where the great tree under which Ayesha preached her pilgrimage is dead, 'or close to death', the fields 'barren as the desert', and the gardens 'in which, long ago, he first saw a beautiful young girl, had long ago yellowed into ugliness'. He takes to his rocking chair and prepares for death. Then on 'the last night of his life' he realizes that the tree is burning: 'He saw the tree explode into a thousand fragments, and the trunk crack, like a heart.' He himself falls in 'the withered dust', but as he does so he feels something brushing his lips and sees 'the little cluster of butterflies struggling to enter his mouth' – butterflies, the symbols of resurrection that have fed and clothed Ayesha from her first appearance.

Then the sea poured over him, and he was in the water beside Ayesha, who had stepped miraculously out of his wife's body...'- Open,' she was crying. 'Open wide!' Tentacles of light were flowing

85

from her navel and he chopped at them, chopped, using the side of his hand. 'Open,' she screamed. 'You've come this far, now do the rest.'

He does the rest: 'His body split open from his adam's-apple to his groin' (exactly the image Allie Cone had used, we recall, to express her fear of love: the fear of being opened 'from your adam's apple to your crotch' (*SV* 314)), 'so that she could reach deep within him, and now she was open, they all were, and at the moment of their opening the waters parted, and they walked to Mecca across the bed of the Arabian Sea'. It is an extraordinary, concentrated image of birth, death, and resurrection, with the fact of human love and sexuality as the hinge that attaches us to these ultimate things – things that we can never 'understand', but only perceive as mysteries. And it is to religion, revelation, as well as to art, that we may look for a witness to their significance. The reader who has come so far may well wonder that the charge of blasphemy should be laid against such writing, and might rather share the view put cogently by Fawzia Afzal-Khan:

> the point of view that emerges is not anti-Islam but anti-closure, opposed, in principle, to any dualistic, fixed way of looking at things. Framed in this way, Rushdie's impulse towards blasphemy becomes really an impulse towards regeneration: renewal born of a destruction of old, fixed ways of seeing and understanding.[13]

How to come down from such exaltation to the ubiquitous 'real world'? Joyce manages this with the switch from the epiphanies to sombre realism in the *Portrait*; and Rushdie does it here to provide his own real-world conclusion. We switch from London – and from the Arabian Sea – to Bombay, eighteen months later, where both Gibreel Farishta and Saladin Chamcha have separately returned. Gibreel has come back to resume his film career, Saladin to be with his dying father; in fact, to 'fall in love with [his] father' again, and to recover 'many old, rejected selves' (*SV* 523). Then Allie Cone arrives *en route* for a mountaineering expedition, and Saladin becomes uneasy. He has a strange sense of being haunted, again; a feeling that 'the shades of his imagination were stepping out into the real world, that destiny was acquiring the slow, fatal logic of a dream' (*SV* 540). Allie dies in a fall from Gibreel's apartment, just as Rekha

Merchant had done. Gibreel arrives at Chamcha's house in a distracted state to tell his story – which begins with a familiar formula: 'Kan ma kan/Fi qadim azzaman...It was so it was not in a time long forgot' (*SV* 544), the take-it-and-leave-it palinode on which all story floats – whether as enchanted sea or miasmal ocean. The substance of Gibreel's ravings is a series of snatches from earlier in the novel, including of course Saladin's own obscene 'satanic verses' multi-voiced over the telephone that drove him out of his mind. In the logic of the novel, one of them has to die; and it is Gibreel who pulls a pistol from the magic lamp and puts it in his mouth. All that is left is for Saladin to look out, from this side, at the Arabian Sea, on which the full moon makes a pathway 'like a parting in the water's shining hair, like a road to miraculous lands'. His own story, however, needs no miracle. His father is dead; but his woman, Zeeny Vakil, is at his elbow: 'he was getting another chance.' And, as in Joyce's last novel, *The Satanic Verses* then puts its own tail in its mouth: 'If the old refused to die, the new could not be born' (*SV* 546–7).

The Satanic Verses is a big novel in every sense: geographically (it has been called 'a tale of three cities'), temporally (ranging from the seventh century to the twentieth), philosophically (the sophisticated but unaffected engagement with an encyclopaedia of ideas), culturally (in the different traditions with which it interacts), linguistically (there are six languages used in its composition). But it is as an exploration of the alternatives of faith and doubt that it has made the greatest impact – if these are actually alternatives. St Augustine said, *credo quia impossible est*: I believe because it is impossible to believe. This is the Augustine whose *Confessions* are one of the permanent tributaries of fiction; who is acknowledged as one of the architects of modern consciousness. And perhaps we should understand Rushdie's troublesome novel (like Henry II's troublesome priest, Thomas Becket, prime mover of another pilgrimage) as a pilgrimage into the imagination in search of the source of religious feeling – however ambivalent its findings are. From first page to last, this is its true trajectory. No novel so obsessed by the temptation of faith can be judged as 'blasphemous'. The only worlds that are seriously called into question in Rushdie's fiction are the flattened, value-free world of contemporary culture, wherever this may be found in its various conditions of exhaustion; and also the world of terror, whether this serves a secular ideology or whether (as often) it conceals itself behind a religious imagination that has been perverted and usurped in the pursuit of political power.

APPENDIX: THE RUSHDIE AFFAIR

Occasional reference only has been made in this study to the wider political response to *The Satanic Verses*, as this has intersected with legitimate criticism of the novel. But the wider response is also part of the story, and I will attempt to provide here an outline of the complicated events and issues that have become known as the Rushdie Affair. (For references and further reading, see the relevant section of the Select Bibliography.)

The Satanic Verses was published in London by Viking on 26 September 1988. There were immediate protests in India against what was understood from reports (and from an interview with Rushdie published in *India Today* on 15 September under the heading 'My Theme is Fanaticism') to be a work that offered insult to Islam, and the novel was banned in India in October. Bans followed in South Africa (October), Bangladesh and Sudan (November), Sri Lanka (December), and Pakistan (February 1989); very soon it was proscribed throughout the Islamic world. In the UK an Action Committee on Islamic Affairs was founded to mobilize public opinion against the novel; there was a protest rally in London, followed by demonstrations in other British cities. On 14 January a copy of *The Satanic Verses* was burnt on the streets of Bradford, attracting widespread media attention. On 12 February six people were killed during anti-Rushdie riots in Islamabad. The climax to the protests occurred on 14 February 1989, when the Ayatollah Homeini of Iran (whose period in exile during the reign of the Shah is referred to in the novel: see pp. 205–15) issued a fatwa or religious edict, sentencing Salman Rushdie to death for blasphemy, under Islamic law; enjoining Muslims everywhere to carry out the sentence, offering the double incentive of martyrdom and a large material reward. With little choice, Rushdie accepted the offer of police protection, and went into hiding. Homeini himself died four months later, but hardliners seized on this fact to insist that the *fatwa* was irreversible; and indeed it was reiterated at intervals from Tehran. For ten years, until the peacemaking statement by the Iranian Government in September 1998, Salman Rushdie remained a fugitive from an archaic system of arbitrary punishment; a situation which, as he conceded during that time, seemed uncannily to have entangled him in his own fictions: 'It is hard to express how it feels to have attempted to portray an objective reality and then to have become its subject' (*IH* 404).[14]

The Committee for the Defence of Salman Rushdie and his Publishers was set up one week after the *fatwa*, to organize resistance, and has maintained a detailed chronology of events from 'Day 1', published under the title 'Fiction, fact and the *fatwa*' in *The Rushdie Letters* (1993).[15] Here are listed the most significant events: including, alarmingly, the violence. The six deaths in Islamabad, already mentioned; the deaths of twelve Muslim rioters, shot by police in Bombay on 24 February 1989; the death of a security guard, killed in a bomb attack on the British Council library in Karachi four days later; another death and more injuries as a result of confrontations in Dhaka and Kharachi in March. Later the same month, two Muslim leaders who had spoken in Rushdie's defence are shot and killed in Belgium. Naguib Mahfouz receives death threats; there are attacks on bookshops in England and abroad. Two years on, on 3 July 1991, the Italian translator of *The Satanic Verses*, Ettore Capriolo, is stabbed by an Iranian in Milan. A week later, the Japanese translator Hitoshi Igarashi is stabbed to death in Tokyo. There is no let-up. In September 1993 the Norwegian publisher of the novel, Wilhelm Nygaard, is shot and severely wounded.

Despite this terroristic atmosphere – indeed, fuelled by a general revulsion at the idea of a death sentence being passed on a British citizen, as it were *urbi et orbi*, by a foreign power – there is a growing platform of support. First official support, from the UK Government, the governments of all the EC countries, the UN, and UNESCO, whose Director-General, Federico Mayor, identifies 'a sense of loss whenever the human imagination is condemned to silence'. The American Senate passes a resolution condemning the threats against Rushdie, and there are statements of support from other American sources. Sir Sridath Ramphal, Secretary-General of the

Commonwealth Secretariat, reminds Iran of the boundaries of diplomatic behaviour: 'Even countries that have banned the book's publication draw the line at incitement to the author's assassination.' European writers, journals, newspapers, keep the matter in the forefront of debate; France is especially active. Wole Soyinka defends 'the creative world' against censorship; it has 'the will and the resources and the imagination' to resist. Developing out of an ICA conference in London in March, *The Rushdie File* is published in September; this catalogues worldwide support for Rushdie and his novel from writers and intellectuals – though not without some questioning and some dissenting voices. On the first anniversary of the *fatwa*, Harold Pinter reads Rushdie's lecture 'Is Nothing Sacred?' to the ICA in London. On 30 September 1990 Rushdie is interviewed by Melvyn Bragg on BBC Television's prime-time *South Bank Show*. On 'Day 1,000', American PEN organizes a demonstration in New York. On the third anniversary, Rushdie makes an appearance at an event in London hosted by the Friends of Salman Rushdie, attended by Günther Grass, Tom Stoppard, and Martin Amis, with videoed statements from Edward Said, Nadine Gordimer, Seamus Heaney, and Derek Walcott.

One of the most problematic episodes was Rushdie's decision, in December 1990, to 'embrace Islam' – announced in an article in *The Times* on 28 December. Here he professed 'an intellectual understanding of religion', and offered some concessions (including the suspension of plans for a paperback edition of his novel). This decision had been taken on the advice of Islamic scholars who had suggested such a move might defuse the international tension. But no such reciprocation occurred (as the July 1991 attacks illustrated), and Rushdie was forced to realize he had made a mistake – incurring criticism on both sides. Almost inevitably, he had to renege on this 'conversion', which he did in an address at Colombia University on 12 December 1991, concluding with the defiant assertion: 'Free speech is life itself.'[16] The much-disputed paperback edition was eventually published (by an anonymous 'Consortium') on 24 March 1992.

Inevitably, discussion of the Rushdie Affair over the last ten years has provided the opportunity for much airing of prejudice, self-righteous moralizing, and even the settling of personal scores; which are no doubt best ignored. But some arguments need to be rehearsed. One thinks particularly of the attitude of those who, focusing on that part of the novel (the larger part) set in Britain, questioned the right of an immigrant author like Rushdie to criticize his adopted society in such uncompromising terms. This parallels the doubts expressed earlier by some critics as to his legitimacy as a commentator on those societies (India and Pakistan) he had left behind – doubts that have been considered in earlier chapters of this study. Both arguments are based upon the mistaken, mechanical assumption that a writer must be a paid-up member of a religion, group, or nation – complicit, accommodated – in order to earn the right to testify. Such an idea, one reflects, would disqualify many other twentieth-century writers: Conrad, Joyce, Lawrence (abroad), Hemingway, Orwell (in Spain), Kundera (in France), and so on. In fact, almost the opposite of this defensive reflex is true. Paradoxically perhaps, betrayal (in the conventional sense – that is, the exposure of one's own inherited pieties to criticism, even to ridicule) is almost a writer's duty. As Joyce's Stephen Dedalus puts it: 'You talk to me of nationality, language, religion. I shall try to fly by those nets.'[17]

The more significant debate has focused on the issue of free speech. Rushdie has declared himself a free-speech absolutist, and this is consistent with Article 19 of the Universal Declaration of Human Rights: 'Everyone has the right of freedom of opinion and expression; this right includes freedom to hold opinions without interference and to seek, receive and impart information and ideas through any media and regardless of frontiers.' But, as has been pointed out, this article is always quoted, misleadingly, out of any relevant context (even without the qualifying Article 20 that follows). Simon Lee has argued in *The Cost of Free Speech*, a book prompted by the Rushdie Affair among other issues, that the free-speech argument is usually mishandled by those who are unwilling to ponder its real complexities and contradictions – which are not helped by imprecise and inconsistent provisions in law. ('The *law*...has been exposed as hopelessly confused by the Rushdie affair.')[18] This relates especially to the present law of blasphemy in Britain, which only protects the Christian religion – a reasonable cause for grievance in the Muslim community. (A private prosecution of the novel was rejected on precisely these grounds in March 1989.[19]) This is a theme also of Richard Webster's *A Brief History of Blasphemy*, subtitled *Liberalism, Censorship, and 'The Satanic Verses'*.[20] It is significant that both Lee and Webster are consistently critical of the one-sided way in which the free-speech issue has been used by Rushdie's supporters, to the disadvantage of minority groups.

But the law can only try to create the level playing field; it cannot dictate the rules of the game. The problem remains the cultural one of mutual incomprehension. Lee suggests that the 'final lesson of the Rushdie affair for our debate on free speech is that it is bound up in our understanding of the differences between various modes of discourse'.[21] Religious, cultural, and political discourses simply do not interface in the global village. Rhetoric and *realpolitik* – or fiction and fact; imagination and material conditions – are programmed for conflict on a whole range of issues.[22] And so, whereas Rushdie and his supporters (of whom I count myself one) have the right and duty to argue their case, this must include a recognition that the very terms of the argument will make their conclusions unacceptable, even incomprehensible, to others.

Which brings us back to blasphemy: one of those archaic, untranslatable words. The perception of blasphemy arises at the fault-lines of discourse, where one system of values and beliefs conflicts with another outside the tolerance levels normally observed. (Malise Ruthven alludes in his sympathetic study of the case to 'the gulf between Islamic and Christian values'.[23]) Reading *The Satanic Verses* on its own terms, as I have tried to do in the foregoing chapter, it is hard to understand the grounds for real offence. But, like the retina, the imagination itself has its blind spots. Trying to compensate for these, it should not be impossible to understand how a different structure of consciousness might find such a radical exercise in scepticism as the novel conducts to be intolerable, even repugnant. Ruthven identifies 'religious doubt' as 'the central condition of modernity';[24] it should be no surprise that many will resist the condition. The communications problem is real, and must be admitted as such; there may be good faith (as well as the other kind) on both sides of the question. But what cannot be admitted, ever, as a consequence of this, is the right of anyone to short-circuit the argument by threatening the life of an antagonist. In an observation cited by Lee, a Supreme Court judge argued in a censorship case from 1927 that 'the remedy to be applied is more speech, not enforced silence'.[25] More speech, more evidence, more argument, more criticism; more activity, that is to say, in what Rushdie has called 'the arena of discourse...where the struggle of languages can be acted out' (IH 427).

Now that the Iranian Government has dissociated itself from the infamous fatwa, we can hope not only that Salman Rushdie may be returned to his life, but that the novel at the epicentre of the Affair may be returned to this arena of discourse.[26]

6

Haroun and the Sea of Stories and *East, West*

HAROUN AND THE SEA OF STORIES

Like many a fairy tale, Rushdie's *Haroun and the Sea of Stories* explores complex moral and philosophical questions in a simple way: via the elementary emblematic of narrative. The misfortunes of Haroun's father, Rashid, who loses his storytelling gift when challenged by literal questions, and the adventures of Haroun himself among mythological beasts, evil demons, supernatural seas, and magical landscapes, are a fictive reflection of real problems in the real world. It is not surprising, therefore, that the novel may be read at one level as a coded account of Rushdie's personal predicament after the *fatwa* – a reading encouraged by the acrostic reference to his son Zafar that appears as dedication:

> Zembla, Zenda, Xanadu,
> All our dream-worlds may come true.
> Fairy lands are fearsome too.
> As I wander far from view
> Read, and bring me home to you.

Rushdie told James Fenton, in interview, that he had promised his son 'the next book I wrote would be one he might enjoy reading'.[1] The details of the coded reading may easily be sketched out: the separation of the family, the attack on free speech ('the greatest Power of all' (*HSS* 119)) by Khattam-Shud, the embodiment of silence and negation; the sinister power of Bezaban, the idol of black ice. A glossary lists names that 'have been derived from Hindustani words', and Bezaban is given as 'Without-a-Tongue' (*HSS* 217). But obviously this reading, while legitimate (even inevitable), risks being reductive.[2] *Haroun* is also

94

a story about story itself, about the need and the capacity of human beings to communicate with each other, across time and across cultures – and despite whatever other obstacles may be put in their way. In this respect, *Haroun* may also be compared with *Gulliver's Travels*, a fiction which is both available to a contextualized, 'local' decoding in terms of eighteenth-century political personalities and events but also floats free of this encumbrance on a sea of its own, a mythical, magical, and dehistoricized account of human behaviour that retains nevertheless an important moral dimension.

It will be interesting, therefore, to consider how *Haroun* offers its own simplified version of Rushdie's recurrent themes. To begin with, the novel provides us with an elementary theory of narrative, communicated in terms of the central metaphor of the 'sea of stories'. This sea is located, we discover, on the invisible, elliptical moon Kahani, the orbit of the imagination (the word simply means 'story'), and is fed by a wellspring that constitutes a powerfully positive image: 'a huge underwater fountain of shining white light' (*HSS* 167). This fountain has immediate analogies in the romantic imagery of Blake and Coleridge (who is quoted in the text); but there are more archaic sources, first in the Sanskrit *Kathasaritsagara* or 'ocean of the stream of stories' referred to in *Midnight's Children* and then to Ganga, the queen among rivers, in the *Ramayana*, which is invoked for its healing properties by Ansurmat near the beginning of the poem. This magical sea is the source of all story, as Haroun's father assures him, introducing his son to the metaphor that will be literalized in the narrative that follows. Sailing on the sea later, Haroun is able to observe for himself its emblematic qualities:

> He looked into the water and saw that it was made up of a thousand thousand thousand and one different currents, each one a different colour, weaving in and out of one another like a liquid tapestry of breathtaking complexity; and Iff explained that these were the Streams of Story, that each coloured strand represented and contained a single tale. Different parts of the Ocean contained different sorts of stories, and as all the stories that had ever been told and many that were still in the process of being invented could be found here, the Ocean of the Streams of Story was in fact the biggest library in the universe. (*HSS* 72)

The beauty of stories is that they are (like water itself) recyclable.

As his guide Iff the Water-Genie tells Haroun – in what is a very creditable version of the origins of narrative, and a good summary of what Rushdie has argued in discursive contexts elsewhere – 'Nothing comes from nothing... no story comes from nowhere; new stories are born from old – it is the new combinations that make them new.' And it is the success of Rushdie's recycling that it can retain fidelity to its ancient sources, the pristine quality, while at the same time incorporating contemporary references: as here, to Borges's story 'The Library of Babel'.[3] In answer to Haroun's question about turbulence, Butt the Hoopoe contributes his own narratological formula: 'Any story that is worth its salt can handle a little shaking up' (HSS 86, 79); and it is up to the Floating Gardeners (one of the more delightful inventions in the book) to ensure that the strands do not get too tangled. These principles are enough to justify the wholesale recasting of 'half-familiar stories' by the entertaining (and, as it turns out, cross-dressed) page-boy Blabbermouth.[4]

However, the sea of stories and its subscribers, professional storytellers like Rashid, have more to worry about than turbulence. There is a plot abroad systematically to poison the sea, and even to plug the wellspring itself. The author of this plot is the sinister Khattam-Shud, introduced as 'the Arch-Enemy of all Stories, even of Language itself... the Prince of Silence and the Foe of Speech', and later revealed to be none other than the Cultmaster himself, high priest of the idol Bezaban (HSS 39, 101). He is the principle of negation, announcing that '*for every story there is an anti-story*': 'There he sits at the heart of darkness... and he eats light, eats it raw with his bare hands' (HSS 160, 145). Khattam-Shud's hostility to stories is for reasons that would be described in the real world as ideological – as he explains in response to Haroun's question as to why he hates stories so much, since for him they are 'fun':

> 'The world, however, is not for Fun,' Khattam-Shud replied. 'The world is for Controlling.'
> 'Which world?' Haroun made himself ask.
> 'Your world, my world, all worlds,' came the reply. 'They are all there to be Ruled. And inside every single story, inside every Stream in the Ocean, there lies a world, a story-world, that I cannot Rule at all. And that is the reason why.' (HSS 161)

Rushdie's metaphor lends itself to ecological elaboration, as with Haroun's analysis of the polluted waters around Khattam-Shud's shadow-ship, the huge black 'ark' (like a rogue oil tanker) that actually manufactures poison:

> The thick, dark poison was everywhere now, obliterating the colours of the Streams of Story, which Haroun could no longer tell apart. A cold, clammy feeling rose up from the water, which was near freezing point, 'as cold as death', Haroun found himself thinking. Iff's grief began to overflow. 'It's our own fault,' he wept. 'We are the Guardians of the Ocean, and we didn't guard it. Look at the Ocean, look at it! The oldest stories ever made, and look at them now. We let them rot, we abandoned them, long before this poisoning. We lost touch with our beginnings, with our roots, our Wellspring, our Source....' (*HSS* 146)

They are alerted to this situation by Haroun's nightmare, a perverted version of 'Princess Rescue Story Number S/1001/ZHT/420/41(r)xi', which he endures after drinking polluted water from the sea. '"It's pollution," said the Water-Genie gravely. "Don't you understand? Something, or somebody, has been putting filth into the Ocean. And obviously if filth gets into the stories, they go wrong"' (*HSS* 73–5).

The celebratory and confirmatory tone of *Haroun* requires that Khattam-Shud should ultimately be perceived as a comic grotesque, a pantomime figure. This outcome is cleverly plotted, in that he is identified at the end with the contemptible clerk Mr Sengupta, whose distinguishing feature is that he has 'no imagination at all', whose mean-minded literalism temporarily disrupts the happy Khalifa family, but who is finally sent packing: 'What a skinny, scrawny, snivelling, drivelling, mingy, stingy, measly, weaselly clerk! As far as I'm concerned he's finished with, done for, gone for good' (*HSS* 210). However, he does also function as a potent reminder of real evil in the real world, the kind of fanaticism that begins in division and ends in cruelty and terror. It is in the principle of division itself, the rigorous and destructive separating out of what should be complementary qualities, that Rushdie locates the real 'poison', here as elsewhere in his fiction. At one point Haroun observes the warrior Mudra 'fighting *against his own shadow*', a memorable image of disintegration, the negation of the true multi-dimensionality of experience – variously realized here in terms of bright versus dark, warm versus freezing, sociability, chatter, and noise versus isolation, silence, and shadow. 'It was a war between Love (of the Ocean, or the Princess) and Death (which was what the Cultmaster Khattam-Shud had in mind for the Ocean, and for the Princess, too).' Mudra explains that Khattam-Shud has taken this division to its extreme: 'he has separated himself from his Shadow!', and can therefore *be in two places at once'* (*HSS* 123, 125, 133). This is a more concrete example of the schizoid metaphysics of Gibreel Farishta in *The Satanic Verses*, who comes to believe (we may recall) that good and evil are not compounded together but entirely separate, the fruit of 'two different trees'.

But Haroun's reflections take him beyond this bifurcated image to a vision of reintegration which is again consistent with Rushdie's own mature thinking on the subject.

> 'But it's not as simple as that,' he told himself, because the dance of the Shadow Warrior showed him that silence had its own grace and beauty (just as speech could be graceless and ugly); and that Action could be as noble as Words; and that creatures of darkness could be as lovely as the children of the light. 'If Guppees and Chupwalas didn't hate each other so,' he thought, 'they might actually find each other pretty interesting. Opposites attract, as they say.' (*HSS* 125)

And this is exactly what is allowed to happen at the end. When the sun rises for the first time over Gup City, it destroys the 'super-computers and gigantic gyroscopes that had controlled the behaviour of the Moon, in order to preserve the Eternal Daylight and the Perpetual Darkness and the Twilight Strip in between'; Kahani becomes 'a sensible Moon...with sensible days and nights' (*HSS* 172, 176). And, when 'Peace [breaks] out', it is marked by a series of reunions – of Night and Day, Speech and Silence, which 'would no longer be separated into Zones by Twilight Strips and Walls of Force'; and of course, by the reunion of the Khalifa family itself (*HSS* 191, 210).

The question that destabilized the 'happy beginning' of *Haroun* was Mr Sengupta's querulous complaint, 'What's the use of stories that aren't even true?': which is first swallowed by Soraya, Rashid's wife, and then fatally repeated to Rashid by his son Haroun. Haroun cannot 'get the terrible question out of his head', and is perplexed by his own reflections on truth and lies:

Nobody ever believed anything a politico said, even though they pretended as hard as they could that they were telling the truth. (In fact, this was how everyone knew they were lying.) But everyone had complete faith in Rashid, because he always admitted that everything he told them was completely untrue and made up out of his own head. (*HSS* 20)

The trouble is that Rashid loses faith in himself. One of Haroun's favourites among his father's stories is that of Moody Land: 'the story of a magical country that changed constantly, according to the moods of its inhabitants. In Moody Land, the sun would shine all night if there were enough joyful people around ... - when people got angry the ground would shake; and when people were muddled or uncertain about things the Moody Land got confused as well.' Moody Land sounds like the natural habitat of the 'pathetic fallacy', whereby we project our emotions onto our environment. But in the chill mist of the Dull Lake, Rashid is suddenly made to see it *as* fallacious. ' "The Moody Land was only a story, Haroun," Rashid replied. "Here we're somewhere real." When Haroun heard his father say *only a story*, he understood that the Shah of Blah was very depressed indeed, because only deep despair could have made him say such a terrible thing'. (*HSS* 48).

Rushdie's own fairy tale provides, in its own terms, an answer to Mr Sengupta's blank, banal, and reductive question. The answer is that truth and falsehood, reality and fiction – 'the Frontiers of Height and Depth,' as Swift has it – 'border upon each other',[5] and cannot be simply lined up in opposition like the black and white pieces on a chessboard – the chessboard, we may remember, that is rejected as too simple a metaphor for human experience in *Midnight's Children*; and that turns up again here in Haroun's polluted dream.[6] The positive and optimistic formula that first enables Haroun to take issue with his father's depression, and his capitulation to the 'real world' of the Dull Lake, is what the reader carries back from Kahani, as Haroun himself brings back as talisman the model of his magical bird: 'the real world was full of magic, so magical worlds could easily be real' (*HSS* 50). Which takes us, via the Land of Oz, to Rushdie's collection of short stories.

EAST, WEST

Of the nine stories included in the collection *East, West*, the first six had been published previously in a number of different journals (the earliest in 1981). One can hardly expect the same degree of coherence from this collection, therefore, as from a novel – even a Rushdie novel. But the arrangement of the stories into three groups of three – East; West; and East, West (the three unpublished stories) – addresses directly the facts (and fictions) of cultural difference, misunderstanding, and antagonism; and it is under this aspect that the stories will first be considered here.[7] The title is one half of an English proverbial saying – 'East, West, Home's Best' – on which this collection (indeed, a good part of Rushdie's work) is an ironic commentary. The proverb itself can be interpreted in at least two ways: 'whether you travel to the east or the west, home (back in England) is best': this is the nineteenth-century imperialist xenophobic reading. Or (the twentieth-century post-colonial, culturally pluralist reading): 'whether you live in the east or the west, your home there is the best place to be.' But there is a third reading – we might I suppose call this the postmodern or post-fatwah version – which is articulated by Rushdie at the end of his booklet on the film *The Wizard of Oz* (written for the British Film Institute in 1992). Rushdie loves the film but hates the ending, where Dorothy accepts the Good Witch Glinda's suggestion that 'there's no place like home':

> How does it come about, at the close of this radical and enabling film ... that we are given this conservative little homily? Are we to believe that Dorothy has learned no more on her journey than that she didn't need to make such a journey in the first place? Must we accept that she now accepts the limitations of her home life, and agrees that the things she doesn't have there are no loss to her? *'Is that right?'* Well, excuse *me*, Glinda, but is it hell.

Rushdie offers us, in his conclusion, his own 'little homily' instead, premised on the interesting fact that, in the sixth of the thirteen Oz books that Frank Baum wrote following the success of the *Wizard*, Dorothy actually goes back to Oz with Auntie Em and Uncle Henry and becomes a princess (as all little girls should, given the right circumstances).

So Oz finally *became* home; the imagined world became the actual world, as it does for us all, because the truth is that once we have left our childhood places and started out to make up our lives, armed only with what we have and are, we understand that the real secret of the ruby slippers is not that 'there's no place like home', but rather that there is no longer any such place *as* home: except, of course, for the home we make, or the homes that are made for us, in Oz: which is anywhere, and everywhere, except the place from which we began.   (WO 56–7)

The themes of homelessness and making a home are explored in *East, West* in several different ways. First through the number of 'displaced persons', otherwise migrants, who actually feature in the stories. Everybody seems to live anywhere else except where they were born. Indians and Pakistanis are self-exiled in London; alongside them is a retired Grand Master from Hungary. 'Exiles, displaced persons of all sorts, even homeless tramps have turned up for a glimpse of the impossible' in 'At the Auction of the Ruby Slippers'. Nor is this exclusively a contemporary experience; in the third of the 'West' stories, for example, Columbus languishes in exile at the court of Queen Isabella of Spain, her 'invisible man', the exotic foreigner who lends her court *'a certain cosmopolitan tone'*; meanwhile he has to console himself with those dreams and 'possibilities' that only 'the harsh . . . ties of history' will eventually cause to materialize (*EW* 107–19). The migrants' difficulty with language itself underlines this alienation – a feature which is strongly marked in the last group of three stories, 'East, West', where cultures blend and clash. In 'The Courter', the *ayah* is known as 'Certainly-Mary' and her Hungarian admirer as 'Mixed-Up' for precisely this reason; they are adrift in a tongue foreign to both of them. Though this does have its advantages:

English was hard for Certainly-Mary, and this was a part of what drew damaged old Mixed-Up towards her. The letter p was a particular problem, often turning into an f or a c; when she proceeded through the lobby with a wheeled wicker shopping basket, she would say, 'Going shocking,' and when, on her return, he offered to help lift the basket up the front ghats, she would answer, 'Yes, fleas.'   (EW 176)

It is by this logic that the porter becomes the courter, and their relationship is adventitiously defined. The narrator's more shadowy father has his own problems, too; on one occasion he is slapped by an assistant in a chemist's shop when he asks for 'nipples' rather than teats (*EW* 176, 184). The characters in 'Chekov and Zulu' have come by their nicknames likewise through an accident of language, mishearing the name 'Sulu' from *Star Trek*; not even from *Star Trek* direct, but from the series recycled on the radio from 'cheap paperback novelizations': 'No TV to see it on, you see. The whole thing was just a legend wafting its way from the US and UK to our lovely hill-station of Dehra Dun' (*EW* 165). The conversation in Zulu's house in Wembley is hardly North London patois, either. But despite these displacements, in only one story does anyone actually follow Dorothy and go back home. This consolation is reserved for the 70-year-old *ayah* we have met as Certainly-Mary, whose life has been used up anyway in service abroad. And even here, the 'culturally plural' narrator (who has just been issued with his British passport) undercuts her decision, by refusing to choose between the cultural offerings available.

> the passport did, in many ways, set me free. It allowed me to come and go, to make choices that were not the ones my father would have wished. But I, too, have ropes around my neck, I have them to this day, pulling me this way and that, East and West, the nooses tightening, commanding, *choose, choose*.
> I buck, I snort, I whinny, I rear, I kick. Ropes, I do not choose between you, Lassoes, lariats, I choose neither of you, and both. Do you hear? I refuse to choose. (*EW* 211)

The cultural question remains unanswered – on what is, significantly enough, the last page of the last story, with the strands left deliberately untied.

A second theme that unites these stories is that developed in Chapter 1 of this study, and conveniently summarized in Rushdie's critique of *Oz*: how 'the imagined world [becomes] the actual world', how the self is constructed out of the confrontation with circumstance. Six of the stories will furnish examples here – often, as we shall see, of relative failure in the task of self-making. Ramani the rickshaw-wallah in 'Free Radio' has 'the rare quality of total belief in his dreams', but this only makes him vulnerable to the persuasion of the 'thief's widow' he lives with (another fictional embodiment of Mrs Gandhi) to accept the free radio in exchange for his right of reproduction.

As the narrator tells him, 'My idiot child, you have let that woman deprive you of your manhood!' Ramani never even gets his radio, but goes to Bombay, from where he writes letters full of fantasy about a new career in the movies, persisting with 'the huge mad energy which he had poured into the act of conjuring reality', and with which he has conspired (ironically) to cheat himself of his own future (*EW* 19–32). 'The Prophet's Hair' is another fiction about how fiction – this time, in the form of superstitious belief – can ravage ordinary human life. The circumstances surrounding the theft, finding, and restealing of a relic destroy a merchant's family: in a single catastrophic paragraph, he stabs his daughter (by mistake) and falls on his sword in remorse, for his wife to be 'driven mad by the general carnage' and committed to an asylum. But the relic is returned and authenticated: 'It sits to this day in a closely guarded vault by the shores of the loveliest of lakes in the heart of the valley which was once closer than any other place on earth to Paradise' (*EW* 55–7). The discrepancy between the untroubled, pellucid prose in which this story is narrated (suggested by the phrase that describes the family before their misadventure, enjoying a 'life of porcelain delicacy and alabaster sensibilities') and the savagery of its subject matter makes its own formal comment.

The best-known story in the collection, 'At the Auction of the Ruby Slippers', is especially interesting in this connection because it derives from a real circumstance and then spirals off to make its point about imaginative excess. The real circumstance was the auction by MGM in May 1990 of the ruby slippers worn by Judy Garland in the *Wizard of Oz* film. The slippers went, Rushdie tells us, for 'the amazing sum of $15,000. The buyer was, and has remained, anonymous. Who was it who wished so profoundly to possess, perhaps even to wear, Dorothy's magic shoes? Was it, dear reader, you? Was it I?' (*WO* 46). The question generates the story (first printed along with Rushdie's essay), which explores the permeable boundaries between fact and fantasy, desire and its fulfilment. Among the people coming to bid for the slippers are fictional characters: from paintings, novels, and other films, all seeking to make their bids for power – or is it immortality?

> This permeation of the real world by the fictional is a symptom of the moral decay of our post-millennial culture. Heroes step down off

cinema screens and marry members of the audience. Will there be no end to it? Should there be more rigorous controls? Is the State employing insufficient violence? We debate such questions often. There can be little doubt that a large majority of us opposes the free, unrestricted migration of imaginary beings into an already damaged reality, whose resources diminish day by day. After all, few of us would choose to travel in the opposite direction (though there are persuasive reports of an increase in such migrations latterly). (*EW* 94–5)[8]

The slippers are magical currency; they can provide access to everything, the fulfillment of all our wishes and dreams. The narrator is bidding for the slippers himself; he wants their power to win a woman's love. But, as the tension mounts in the saleroom, and the bids themselves spiral away from reality, the narrator is suddenly overtaken by another power: the detachment of pure contemplation, the 'lightness of being' characteristic of fiction itself. 'There is a loss of gravity, a reduction in weight, a floating in the capsule of the struggle. The ultimate goal crosses a delirious frontier. Its achievement and our own survival become – yes! – fictions. And fictions, as I have come close to suggesting before, are dangerous.' Dangerous because they may persuade us to accept the 'damaged reality' described above, or even contribute to it in ways that are suggested in the next paragraph.

In fiction's grip, we may mortgage our homes, sell our children, to have whatever it is we crave. Alternatively, in that miasmal ocean, we may simply float away from our desires, and see them anew, from a distance, so that they seem weightless, trivial. We let them go. Like men dying in a blizzard, we lie down in the snow to rest. (*EW* 102)

This story fulfils, therefore, some of the anxieties about fiction expressed in the essays, how TV and the cinema may impair rather than enhance our sense of reality, how books themselves, and theatre, may distract us with false – which in the order of art means inadequately imagined – ideologies.

There is another health warning against fiction in the first story in the final group, 'Harmony of the Spheres' – a story whose aptly named suicide hero Eliot Crane is a cousin-german of Gibreel Farishta. Crane is a cut-down Faust figure whose 'immersion in the dark arts was more than scholarly': 'Pentangles, illuminati, Maharishi, Gandalf: necromancy was

part of the *zeitgeist*, the private language of the counter-culture.'
He has met a demon. The impressionable Indian narrator Khan
has been initiated by him: 'I was taught the verses that conjured
up the Devil, *Shaitan*, and how to draw the shape that would
keep the Beast 666 confined.' An immigrant at Cambridge, Khan
believes Eliot can help him relocate and reinvent himself.

> in Eliot's enormous, generously shared mental storehouse of the
> varieties of 'forbidden knowledge' I thought I'd found another way
> of making a bridge between here-and-there, between my two
> othernesses, my double unbelonging. In that world of magic and
> power there seemed to exist the kind of fusion of world-views,
> European Amerindian Oriental Levantine, in which I desperately
> wanted to believe.

But Eliot turns out to be a paranoid schizophrenic, slave not
master: 'He couldn't help anyone, the poor sap; couldn't even
save himself. In the end his demons came for him', and he blows
his brains out (*EW* 125–46). The two Indian diplomats in 'Chekov
and Zulu' likewise never manage to disentangle the reality of
their own lives as husbands and fathers from the fiction among
which they grew up: the misapplied names from *Star Trek* are an
index of a more profound (and yes: dangerous) misapprehension.
It is an ironic comment on the mediatization of experience that,
when he is fated to be in Rajiv Gandhi's entourage at the moment
of his assassination, Chekov steps into eternity aboard Captain
Kirk's spacecraft: 'The scene around him vanished, dissolving in a
pool of light, and was replaced by the bridge of the Starship
Enterprise' (*EW* 170). It is just another episode: a 'virtual' death
rather than a real one. Finally, in the last and longest story, 'The
Courter', for all the imaginative defences that may be set up, the
real world reasserts itself unambiguously. The young Indian
narrator grows up in recognizable London, but still at one remove
from social reality not only because of the language barrier (that
affects his family rather than himself) but once again because of
the mediatized world he constructs for himself, composed of pop
songs, hair styles, fashion, and The Flintstones. But history 1960s
style irrupts into this story more decisively, with the assassination
of Kennedy and the race-hate speeches of Enoch Powell on
television ('a vulpine Englishman with a thin moustache and mad
eyes'), and finally the racial attack on his mother and sister that
comes like an awakening slap from the outside world.

Fictions are dangerous. It is as if the regenerative sea of *Haroun* has degenerated here to the 'miasmal ocean' referred to in the 'Ruby Slippers'; as if Khattam-Shud has had his way after all, and poisoned the Sea of Stories. And, if the inference to be drawn from the stories in *East, West* is, therefore, in some respects a negative one, then this may have something to do with the form of the short story itself, which is perhaps not the most congenial means of expression for Rushdie. It does not allow sufficient room for his ideas to stretch and develop, for the tentacular connections to establish themselves. Walter Benjamin remarked that the short story is alien to the oral tradition in that it does not allow 'that slow piling one on top of the other of thin, transparent layers', which image, he suggests, provides 'the most appropriate picture of the way in which the perfect narrative is revealed through the layers of a variety of retellings'.[9] Rushdie has himself observed that, if he has written relatively few short stories, this is because the material that might make a story tends to get swallowed up in the larger system of the novels, which he sees as 'everything books' made up of 'a jostle of stories'; 'and so there's nothing left over for short stories'.[10] And perhaps this is as it should be – as one last instance might confirm. In 'Yorick', a Shakespearean variation which is generally felt to be one of the less successful stories in the collection, the narrator breaks off at one point to remark, 'it's true my history differs from Master CHACKPAW's ... so let the versions of the story co-exist, for there's no need to choose' (*EW* 81). The point is, the writer of short stories *has* to choose, given the constraints of the form. Is this not a case of the novel-as-genie struggling to get out of the short-story-as-bottle? Out into the wider world where faith, hope, and fiction may carry us through; and the greatest of these may after all turn out to be fiction. Which is a possible reading of Rushdie's next novel.

7

The Moor's Last Sigh

Rushdie's first big novel since *The Satanic Verses*, seven years on, was awaited with cautious expectation. His readers had willed Rushdie to carry on writing, to triumph over the adversity of his circumstances, but at the same time there was some doubt expressed as to whether he could possibly recapture the imaginative liberty of his earlier work. And in the event *The Moor's Last Sigh* was published to sympathetic rather than enthusiastic reviews.[1] In the first book to include a section on the novel, Catherine Cundy offers what is (she concedes) a 'largely negative assessment'. The novel has been marked, she feels, by the fact of Rushdie's incarceration, and breathes a stifled, exhausted air as a result; it is in her view 'strangely flat – with the two-dimensionality of a largely cerebral reconstitution of "reality"'.[2] (What work of art, one reflects, is not 'cerebral'?) But it may be that there is something preconditioned about these judgements, as if the novel could not possibly be allowed to succeed, whatever its qualities, since that would somehow contradict the comfortable, common-sense idea we have of the continuity between the writer and the work. (One might note in passing that Cundy's book frequently invokes biographical 'facts' to underpin critical judgements.) It should be possible to respond to the novel on its own terms, without such a reflex. It is an assumption of the present account that Rushdie was able to draw on all his resources as a writer for *The Moor's Last Sigh*; and the argument, that, though it is deliberately refracted through the mirror of art, the novel is as ambitious, as demanding, and as fine as anything he has previously written.

One should first note the continuities with Rushdie's earlier work. *The Moor's Last Sigh* returns to India, but to a different India from that of *Midnight's Children* (or *The Satanic Verses*). This is Spanish/Portuguese India, with a different colonial history; the echoes here are not of The East India Company, Amritsar, Mountbatten, and the Raj, but of Vasco da Gama, the Alhambra, and multicultural Goa with its Jewish and Christian communities. The title alludes to *El ultimo suspiro del Moro*, a hill in southern Spain so named because it was the place from which Boabdil, the last Moorish king of Granada, looked back at the city before going into exile in Africa; while two paintings contend for the same title within the novel as well, reflecting Rushdie's obsession with the idea of the palimpsest, the work of art that overlays another. From Cochin we move to Bombay, which takes over as the city centre of the novel; and, after the Indian plot has run its course, we end up back in southern Spain, as if by a process of imaginative restitution, or recentring; like the rebalancing of a wheel. The novel is once again a family saga, the story this time of the doomed Zogoiby family. As with *Shame*, the text is once again prefaced with a family tree. It is a story of sexual infatuation and betrayal; of conquest, trade, and political intrigue; of religion and religious conflict; of generosity and understanding deformed by intolerance; of spiritual values corrupted by commerce. A story, significantly, that creates within itself (like a pearl) the opaque metaphor of its own making. J. M. Coetzee's review perceptively identifies the specialized figure of *ekphrasis* as central to Rushdie's project: 'the conduct of narrative through the description of imaginary works of art.'[3] The function of Rani Harappa's eighteen shawls from *Shame*, reflecting the history of her husband and her times, is fulfilled here by the paintings of Aurora Zogoiby, Moor's mother, which represent not only the micro-narrative of her family within the macro-narrative of her Indian world, but also the narrative of representation itself – the different styles and genres of painting that an evolving consciousness will come to utilize. And it is not only these paintings that operate in this way. There is a series of ancient blue tiles in the synagogue tended by Moor's Jewish grandmother, 'metamorphic tiles' which themselves have narrative and prophetic qualities. 'Some said that if you explored for long enough you'd find your own story in one of the blue-and-white squares, because the pictures on the tiles could change, were changing, generation by generation, to tell the story of the Cochin Jews' (*MLS* 75–6). It is a novel, finally, that explores (with all the courage of self-interrogation – a process that has, no doubt, been matured by Rushdie's predicament) the ambivalence of our values in all these interlocking spheres.

The first-person narrative by the main character, Moraes Zogioby, known as 'Moor', is itself (as we would expect) foregrounded in its technique. The 'last sigh' of the title implies the first cry at birth, Beckett's *vagitus*, as well as the expiration. 'I am what breathes. I am what began long ago with an exhaled cry, what will conclude when a glass held to my lips remains clear.' It is also the breath with which we articulate words. 'A sigh isn't just a sigh. We inhale the world and breathe out meaning. While we can' (*MLS* 53–4).[4] A natural storyteller, Moor as it were breathes narrative. But his story is actually written under compulsion. The 'story of [his] story', as Henry James puts it,[5] is that at the last stage of his life, in Spain, Moor is imprisoned by the demented painter Vasco Miranda, one of his mother's former lovers and a jealous rival in art, who forces him to write his narrative. 'Every day...he brought me pencil and paper. He had made a Scheherazade of me. As long as my tale held his interest he would let me live' (*MLS* 421). A graphological Scheherazade, one should add, according to the Beckettian model: Molloy is provided with paper for the same purpose by 'this man who...gives me money and takes away the pages'.[6] And so Moor recreates in his cell the complex story of his family. He is the fourth child (and only son) of a prosperous mixed family from Cochin in (then) Portuguese Goa. The genetic admixture is important: Moor describes himself as 'a high-born cross-breed', 'a jewholic-anonymous, a cathjew nut, a stewpot, a mongrel cur...a real Bombay mix'. '*Bastard*', he concludes; 'I like the sound of the word' (*MLS* 5, 104). The family fortune derives on the side of his mother, Aurora da Gama, a Christian, from generations in the spice trade; and on the side of his Jewish father, Abraham Zogoiby, from the illicit sequestration and secret sale of jewels housed in the blue-tiled synagogue. These jewels derive ultimately from Boabdil, king of Granada, who had given them to his Jewish mistress, from whom they have passed down through the Zogoiby family. It is the sale of these jewels that saves the firm from bankruptcy when it is threatened by destructive family feuding and the blockade during the

Second World War; but the jewels are handed over by Abraham's mother only at a price. Rumpelstiltskin's price: the life of Abraham's first son, which is therefore surrendered to an intertextual bargain before he is born. The conduct of trade (which may be taken to include this sinister fairy-tale contract) is a major preoccupation in the novel, and the progressive compromises from the vision and energy of the early traders from Vasco da Gama onwards to the corrupt practices of Abraham Zogoiby himself – which eventually involve money-laundering, drugs, prostitution, and arms dealing – are part of the overall theme of degeneration and betrayal.

Moor is born in 1957, and his narrative takes us up to 1993, as he prepares for death: literally lying out on his tombstone, having nailed the sheets of his stolen narrative to doors and gateposts after his escape from Miranda's madhouse, in an allusion to the publication of Martin Luther's testament. What associates him with the authentic family tree of Rushdie's fictional creations is that he is cursed to be a 'magic child, a time-traveller' (*MLS* 219), who grows and ages at exactly twice the normal speed. Thus he is born only four-and-a-half months after conception (though Rushdie also teases us, as elsewhere, with alternative parental possibilities), and his personal narrative of thirty-six years delivers him up a saddened and wizened septuagenarian. Moor learns about the earlier events in his dynastic story through oral tradition: by listening to the stories of his family and their friends and servants. His parents themselves, his three sisters (Ina, Minnie, and Mynah: to prepare for Moor), his uncle Aires and aunt Carmen, his mother's lover Vasco Miranda, and the one-legged servant Lambajan, all piece together the earlier episodes. And there is, of course, the privileged evidence of his mother's paintings, which provide a commentary on important events in the narrative – and have a further significance for the theory of representation, to which we shall return. Inevitably, for a trading family, the family fortunes are closely involved with public events. The novel includes episodes from the First and Second World Wars, from the political unrest in India during the 1930s, and later in the narrative we encounter again events that featured in *Midnight's Children*: the tempestuous time of independence itself, partition, the language riots, Mrs Gandhi's infamous emergency. But, although the Zogoiby family is therefore 'handcuffed to history' in a similar way to Saleem, and although Rushdie occasionally uses the same devices to achieve the parallelism (thus one of Moor's sisters dies in the Bhopal disaster, and when Sanjay Gandhi is killed in a plane crash Moor tells us 'I, too, was plunged towards catastrophe' (*MLS* 274–6)), the historical details are sketched in much more incidentally here than in the earlier novel: history is not used as 'scaffolding' in the same way.[7] In *Midnight's Children* there was a genuine effect of 'split screen' or double focus, whereas in *The Moor's Last Sigh* Moor's own story and the technique of his telling of it retain our attention much more continuously. The background is a more resonant one, composed of fairytale and folktale, epic and myth; literature and art and philosophy as well as history. It is 'an Indian yarn' (*MLS* 87), and Rushdie expects us to make all the formal concessions implied here. Once again, in the syncretist spirit, there are significant Shakespearian intertexts in the novel, this time mainly *The Merchant of Venice* and *Othello*. And, like the latter play, the novel is much more domestic in focus than any of Rushdie's earlier works. It is this intimacy that generates an intensity of emotion that is also, perhaps, uncharacteristic. Elsewhere in Rushdie the macro-narrative tends to put personal feeling into perspective, but here it is personal feeling that establishes the perspective according to which other things are judged.[8]

At the tormented centre of this personal feeling is Moor himself, the 'magic child' who has been singled out for spectacular disappointments in life: a series of exemplary betrayals that explain the regular references to himself as a Christ figure (he presents his story as a crucifixion from the first page). The first betrayal might be seen as that of nature itself, in his handicap, because not only is he condemned by his abnormal growth-rate to be a 'time-traveller' – which is as bad for living, as it is good for storytelling – but he is also born with a deformed left hand: fingers webbed and bunched into an ugly fist that serves him well in his days with Mainduck's thugs in the Bombay underworld. The next betrayal is that by his 'one true love', Uma Sarasvati, an enigmatic figure who first reciprocates Moor's love and then betrays him: to his friends, and ultimately to his parents. The final and most painful betrayal is that by his parents themselves, who disavow him as a result of Uma's destructive plot and refuse to see him from this point on: his mother, above all, 'who never spoke to me, never made confession, never gave me back what I needed, the certainty of her love' (*MLS* 432). The complicated detective-story plot takes over from this point, complete with hired snoops and contract killers; the note of parody is never far below the surface.[9] Aurora is killed in a fall from the high terrace of her Bombay house, where each year on her birthday she has danced a defiant, secular 'dance against the gods' (*MLS* 315). Or was she pushed? And if so, by whom? Only at the end do we learn that her husband, Abraham Zogoiby, was responsible, Moor's own father, who turns out with typical Rushdie hyperbole to be 'the most evil man that ever lived' (*MLS* 417). As the truth of the picture emerges, Moor is employed by his father's business rival Mainduck in a campaign of violent reprisal (reminiscent more of *Shame* than *Midnight's Children*) which reveals that corruption extends further than was ever imagined, implicating the very structures of government. But a familiar Rushdian apocalypse awaits the big players in this dubious game. There is an explosion that destroys whole buildings in the centre of Bombay, and in the confusion that follows Moor takes off for Spain to avoid arrest. Here, as if sleepwalking into the further ramifications of his own plot, he stumbles into Vasco Miranda's mad world of art – from which he is only saved, at the end, by the fairy-tale splinter of glass that has been lodged in Miranda's murderous heart.

The narrative is deliberately pushed over the edge with parodic reworkings of other plots, constellated with allusions, and refracted through a series of stylistic variations. For Rushdie, this is how narrative works: by accretion, complication, parallelism, inversion. This is his architecture. But at the same time the narrative is intended to deliver something else. *The Moor's Last Sigh* is powered by a nucleus of related ethical ideas, each of which bears closely on the other, and which may be said to subtend the moral preoccupations of the patriarch Francisco da Gama and his son (Moor's uncle) Camoens. These relate to the nature of identity, both racial and personal; to the competition between ideas of singularity and multiplicity; and beyond this to the nature and truth of artistic representation. It is the engagement with identity, the shifting boundaries of the self, that gives the most direct access to these, associated as it is (here as in *The Satanic Verses*) with the fiction-making process itself. Underneath Rushdie's narrative of Spanish India there runs a passionate desire for love and harmony: the transcendence of the single, isolated self in a love that, while being personal and sexual, is also imaginative and inclusive, passing out into the infinite. This ethical dimension is introduced by Francisco da Gama via a scientific theory explicitly derived from Joyce's *Portrait of the Artist*: a science-fiction version of Stephen Dedalus's forge for creating the conscience of his race, whereby a magnetic 'Field of Conscience' is maintained in the atmosphere in response to people's behaviour on earth. Rather like an ethical ozone layer – though it has to be said big holes are blown in this before the end. And, just as Shelley reminded us that ethical behaviour begins with the ability to 'put [oneself] in the place of another and of many others',[10] so too for Rushdie it is in the going beyond the self that we may discover our full human value. The extreme instance of this is in the idea of being flayed: literally, losing the distinguishing and separating skin in a 'naked unity of the flesh' (*MLS* 414). The image is introduced by Francisco's daughter-in-law Carmen as an expression of sexual guilt that longs for ablation: '*flay me flay my skin from my body whole entire and let me start again let me be of no race no name no sex*' (*MLS* 47). But it is taken over by Moor himself, associated with an anatomical illustration he has seen as a child: 'When I was young I used to dream ... of peeling off my skin plaintain-fashion, of going forth naked into the world, like an anatomy illustration from *Encyclopaedia Britannica*, all ganglions, ligaments, nervous pathways and veins, set free from the otherwise inescapable jails of colour, race and clan.' This fantasy of self-forgetting is taken even further, he recalls, in 'another version of the dream' in which he would be able to peel away more than skin, and float free of the body altogether, becoming 'simply an intelligence or a feeling set loose in the world, at play in its fields, like a science-fiction glow which needed no physical form' (*MLS* 136). So far, so good; this reads positively, like a psychedelic trip.

But there are bad trips too. A terrifying, negative version of the image occurs during Moor's incarceration: 'As roaches crawled and mosquitoes stung, so I felt that my skin was indeed coming away from my body, as I had dreamed so long ago that it would. But in this version of the dream, my peeling skin took with it all elements of my personality.' And here in the prison, forced to reflect, he perceives that the source of this annihilation is identical with the source of life: his mother. Hers is the real, psychological violence he translates into such physical terms: 'And when he is flayed, when he is a shape without frontiers, a self without walls, then your hands close about his neck... he is farting out his life, just as once you, his mother, farted him into it' (*MLS* 288). But the image returns in its positive form right at the end, in the lyrical culmination to the novel, a passage that reads almost like an epilogue, where Moor has '*scrambled over rough ground*' to sit on his own tombstone and reflect on the sum of experience that has brought him here: '*Thorns, branches and stones tore at my skin. I paid no attention to these wounds; if my skin was falling from me at last, I was happy to shed that load.*' The terms used here clearly refer to the narrative of Christ's passion and death (immediately before this, the written sheets of Moor's story are 'nailed to the landscape in my wake'), just as Joyce alludes to this in the last paragraph of his story 'The Dead'. The figure of the flayed man is also Christ whipped with thorns in the temple before his crucifixion, fulfilling this other system of reference. And, from his vantage point on the tombstone (which is both spatial and temporal), Moor looks out across the valley to the symbolic Alhambra, where the personal image is taken up in a broader, cross-cultural vision:

> the glory of the Moors, their triumphant masterpiece and their last redoubt. The Alhambra, Europe's red fort, sister to Delhi's and Agra's – the palace of interlocking forms and secret wisdom, of pleasure-courts and water-gardens, that monument to a lost possibility that nevertheless has gone on standing, long after its conquerors have fallen; like a testament to lost but sweetest love, to the love that endures beyond defeat, beyond annihilation, beyond despair; to the defeated love that is greater than what defeats it, to that most profound of our needs, to our need for flowing together, for putting an end to frontiers, for the dropping of the boundaries of the self.   (MLS 433)

The intensely concrete and physical image of flaying (which may contain a reference to Swift's livid image of the woman flayed from *A Tale of a Tub*, as well as to Beckett's character Lemuel who is 'flayed alive by memory' in *Malone Dies*[11]) intersects with the idea of the plurality and malleability of the personality that we have met elsewhere in Rushdie, and which is treated if anything more systematically in this novel. Early on, the personality of his grandfather provides Moor with an example: 'To me, the doublenesses in Grandfather Camoens reveal his beauty; his willingness to permit the coexistence within himself of conflicting impulses is the source of his full, gentle humanness' (*MLS* 32). Francisco's 'Fields of Conscience' have at least forged his son's moral vision; a realization through fictional character of the notion of 'negative capability' which Keats identified in Shakespeare; 'when man is capable of being in uncertainties, Mysteries, doubts, without any irritable reaching after fact and reason.'[12]

The desire for transcendence associated with this image is felt both personally (in love) and politically, in a vision of culture. Moor provides the relevant meditation on love whilst in prison, still suffering from the trauma of Uma Sarasvati's death and his mother's betrayal.

> I wanted to cling to the image of love as a blending of spirits, as mélange, as the triumph of the impure, mongrel, conjoining best of us over what there is in us of the solitary, the isolated, the austere, the dogmatic, the pure; of love as democracy, as the victory of the no-man-is-an-island, two's company Many over the clean, mean, apartheiding Ones. (*MLS* 289)

The terminology used here clearly moves beyond personal love to a more comprehensive vision of understanding. This vision has been articulated earlier by the idealistic Camoens to his daughter Belle. He invites her to imagine, and to help create, '*a new world, Belle, a free country, Belle, above religion because secular, above class because socialist, above caste because enlightened, above hatred because loving, above vengeance because forgiving, above tribe because unifying, above language because many-tongued, above colour because multi-coloured...*'(*MLS* 51). Not surprisingly, Camoens's new world has so far failed to materialize. But it is symbolically represented in Rushdie's novel by the culture of the fabulous Alhambra, where Europe met Africa, Christianity and Judaism met Islam, in pluralist embrace, a rare instance of racial and religious tolerance. *The Moor's Last Sigh* is partly an elegy for that culture, and for the very ideals it represented – the more movingly so for the sense the novel conveys of the impssibility of

115

recreating anything resembling it in twentieth-century India; or, for that matter, of rediscovering its rare virtues anywhere else in the modern world.

Such virtues depend upon a philosophical preference for the plural over the singular, the dialectical over the monologic; a preference that is most consistently expressed through Aurora's paintings. It is the 'torrential reality of India' (*MLS* 45) that awakens her art in the first place, and when Camoens sees the murals she has painted during her solitary confinement he exclaims: 'But it is the great swarm of being itself.' Figures from ancient and modern history consort with hybrids from her own imagination, 'half-woman half-tiger, half-man half-snake...sea-monsters and mountain ghouls'. Vasco da Gama is there, claimed as an ancestor:

> Aurora had composed her giant work in such a way that the images of her own family had to fight their way through this hyper-abundance of imagery, she was suggesting that the privacy of Cabral Island was an illusion and this mountain, this hive, this endlessly metamorphic line of humanity was the truth... (*MLS* 59–60)

Whatever political and personal distractions intervene (and many do), this is the dominant form of her art: 'the mythic–romantic mode in which history, family, politics and fantasy jostled each other like the great crowds at V.T. or Churchgate Stations' (*MLS* 203–4). This is what we might call the Bombay Alhambra, which can only be represented in a mode that includes but goes beyond realism; as Vasco Miranda succinctly declares at one point, 'a canvas is not a mirror' (*MLS* 158). And the principles of Aurora's painting are intended to reflect Rushdie's own practice as a writer. The rich invocation of the Spanish and Portuguese past in the novel, the documentation of the political instability of the inter-war years in India, and the description of modern Bombay ('that super-epic motion picture of a city' (*MLS* 129)) match the detailed description of the paintings, words aspiring to iconicity, within the figure of ekphrasis previously identified.

The paintings at this stage, in her mid-career, are devoted to the effacement of dividing lines: 'the dividing lines between two worlds, became in many of these pictures the main focus'; water, land, and air are allowed to merge as Aurora proposes her own 'political' version of this blending: 'Call it Mooristan . . . Call it Palimpstine.' And the political significance is underlined, as Rushdie develops and exploits the possibilities of his self-reflexive commentary: 'In a way these were polemical pictures, in a way they were an attempt to create a romantic myth of the plural, hybrid nation; she was using Arab Spain to re-imagine India' (MLS 226–7). As is implied here, the idea of the palimpsest provides a key to the novel: both the literal palimpsest (exampled by Aurora's painting 'The Moor's Last Sigh', and also, as it happens, by an actual portrait of Rushdie's mother[13]) and the metaphorical palimpsest, as a 'layering' or re-presentation or disguise of any other kind. Rushdie makes use of this metaphor to describe the corrupt commercial practices of Abraham Zogoiby in a passage which has a more general epistemological bearing – recalling as it does the 'permeation of the real world by the fictional' in the earlier 'Ruby Slippers' story from East, West.

> The city itself, perhaps the whole country, was a palimpsest, Under World beneath Over World, black market beneath white; when the whole of life was like this, when an invisible reality moved phantomwise beneath a visible fiction, subverting all its meanings, how then could Abraham's career have been any different? How could any of us have escaped that deadly layering? How, trapped as we were in the hundred per cent fakery of the real, in the fancy-dress, weeping-Arab kitsch of the superficial, could we have penetrated to the full, sensual truth of the lost mother below? How could we have lived authentic lives? (MLS 184–5).

It is one of the remarkable features of The Moor's Last Sigh that these moral ideas are not only entertained but tested to destruction in the novel. This trial of the limits is conducted through the agency of Uma Sarasvati, the novel's contradictory and equivocating angel–devil. It is Uma whom Moor falls in love with, and who teaches him love's transcendent value; only here can he perceive that love overbalances truth, only here are his belief systems fundamentally (and creatively) challenged: 'I do not believe it; I believe it; I do not believe; I believe; I do not, I do not; I do' (MLS 251–2). But having established her power Uma betrays him in the cruellest way possible – sending his parents a tape-recording of their lovemaking, during which she has tempted him to say unforgiveable things. In the sequel she

117

actually tries to kill him, in a trick suicide pact which is bizarrely bungled and results in her own death when two tablets are swapped after a clash of heads (*MLS* 281): one thinks of the switched swords in the last scene of *Hamlet*. And following up Rushdie's own references to Keats, one might suggest that Uma is more chilling than 'La Belle Dame Sans Merci', the classic *femme fatale*, being more a kind of postmodern Lamia – the snake disguised as a woman. She herself has 'no "authentic" identity' (*MLS* 266), and so, like a cold window distilling vapour, is able to drain other people of theirs. It is significant that when the Zogoiby family meets her at the racecourse 'every one of us had a fiercely held opinion about her, and many of these opinions contradicted each other utterly and were incapable of being reconciled' (*MLS* 243). As such, her very embodiment of plural identity reverses its value – a perception Moor records as a 'bitter parable' in which 'the polarities of good and evil were reversed': 'For in the matter of Uma Sarasvati it had been the pluralist Uma, with her multiple selves, her highly inventive commitment to the infinite malleability of the real, her modernistically provisional sense of truth, who had turned out to be the bad egg; and Aurora had fried her...'(*MLS* 272). For Moor–Othello chaos *has* come again; his intellectual as well as his emotional world is turned upside-down. Uma 'showed me the truth', he says, but it is the kind of truth that is worse than lies – or which confuses these categories in a more powerful drug: 'Whoever and whatever she had been, good or evil or neither or both, it is undeniable that I had loved her' (*MLS* 241, 281).

And for Aurora too there is a convulsion, in her art as well as her politics. From this point on she abandons her hybrid forms, and comes under the influence of the Hindu activist Minto with his dangerous separatist ideas: 'Aurora, that lifelong advocate of the many against the one, had with Minto's help discovered some fundamental verities' (*MLS* 272). In her earlier paintings, her son Moraes has served for Aurora as a symbol for India itself; he has been the centre of her pictorial narrative. 'And I was happy to be there, because the story unfolding on her canvases seemed more like my autobiography than the real story of my life' (*MLS* 227). But this very symbol is now invalidated and reversed, in the 'Moor in Exile' sequence; the personal and the political have been simultaneously betrayed in art.

118

And the Moor-figure: alone now, motherless, he sank into immorality, and was shown as a creature of shadows, degraded in tableaux of debauchery and crime. He appeared to lose, in these last pictures, his previous metaphorical rôle as a unifier of opposites, a standard-bearer of pluralism, ceasing to stand as a symbol – however approximate – of the new nation, and being transformed, instead, into a semi-allegorical figure of decay.

The philosophical conclusion comes in what follows, proof of a dismaying contamination of cultural ideals by personal jealousy and disappointment. 'Aurora had apparently decided that the ideas of impurity, cultural admixture and mélange which had been, for most of her creative life, the closest things she had found to a notion of the Good, were in fact capable of distortion, and contained a potential for darkness as well as for light.' We are returned to the perilous depths of *The Satanic Verses*, where human behaviour becomes frighteningly unreliable and ambiguous, as different motives come into view. Her son now appears to Aurora as a *fleur du mal*; and we have a quotation from Baudelaire to make the point (*MLS* 303).

The renegade painter Vasco Miranda also plays his part in this process of destruction from within. Destroyed by his jealousy of Aurora's talent, he has sold out his own art to commerce, producing a readily consumable 'airport art' that mischievously alludes to Salvador Dali's facile surrealism. But he takes his surname, after all, from Shakespeare's wide-eyed heroine in *The Tempest*, with her wonderment at the promise of new worlds; and, true to this suggestion, he promises on his removal to Spain to recreate 'in his "Little Alhambra", the fabulous multiple culture of ancient al-Andalus' (*MLS* 398). But his 'new society' turns out to be a megalomaniac's prison; and he it is, in the novel's extraordinary penultimate scene, who shoots the lost portrait through the heart for it to bleed with the life blood of the Japanese artist whom he has employed to work on its restoration. She herself plays a symbolic role, both as the disbelieving auditor and innocent victim of Moor's story, and also, through her very name, as a kind of good angel – the spirit of art, and the binding powers of language. 'Her name was a miracle of vowels. Aoi Uë: the five enabling sounds of language...constructed her' (*MLS* 423). So both Uma and Vasco contribute to the novel's real tragedy, 'the tragedy of multiplicity destroyed by singularity, the defeat of the Many by the One' (*MLS* 408).

But there is another, more undermining level of scepticism loose in the novel. It is not only Aurora herself, but her critics (including her son) who are entitled to a judgement of her paintings; and so Moor's developing awareness of the potential for falsity in his mother's pictures – reciprocating her judgement of him – opens up another series of intriguing questions. Although Moor feels at one point, as we have seen, that her pictorial narrative 'seemed more like [his] autobiography than the real story of [his] life', he comes to realize, later, that those of his mother's paintings which are motivated by her jealousy of Uma are themselves perverse, and 'did not necessarily bear the slightest connection to events and feelings and people in the real world' (*MLS* 247). This is a disabling realization for him, as the subject of these paintings, but also for us, as readers of Rushdie's novel; because the question is intended to destabilize the paintings' frame-text in the novel itself. If the paintings can tell lies, then so can any art; and this may explain why at several points in the novel Moor is careful himself to question the truth of elements included in his own narrative. 'I have grave doubts about the literal truth of the story' of the painting *The Moor's Last Sigh*, he tells us; and, whereas he goes on to assure his reader that 'of the truth of these further stories there can be no doubt whatsoever', he adds, in deference to the omnipotent reader, 'it is not for me to judge, but for you' (*MLS* 79, 85). We have to set alongside this the deliberate provocation whereby Rushdie mixes in historical materials with his fiction: as when he implies that Aurora might have had an affair with Nehru – quoting in his text from published letters between Nehru and Mrs Gandhi, which are duly cited in the Acknowledgements; and when he makes a knowing allusion to the critic Homi Bhabha in the name of a purchaser of one of Aurora's paintings (*MLS* 117–18, 435; 419). We also have to consider the implications of inviting characters from his other novels into this one – a manœuvre that might be considered either intriguingly self-reflexive or simply self-indulgent. (In either case, Rushdie would be familiar with such textual migration in the work of the eighteenth-century novelists: we find examples in both Fielding and Smollett). Aadam Sinai turns up from *Midnight's Children* to be adopted by Abraham Zogoiby in preference to his own son, Moor; and Zeeny Vakil from *The Satanic Verses* appears in her role as critic of

Aurora's paintings – and gets killed for her pains, in the cataclysmic explosion at the end. This intertextual trespass poses a curious question: are we meant to wonder what effect this death might have on the Saladin Chamcha in whose company she was left at the end of the earlier novel?

It is not only the discourse of art but the 'ordinary' narrative discourse within the novel that is hedged around with doubts and hesitations and uncertainties. 'It is difficult for me, after all these years, to know what to believe,' Moor confesses as he writes out his story – a sentiment shared by Aoi Uë as she listens to him. It is 'the old biographer's problem: even when people are telling their own life stories, they are invariably improving on the facts' (*MLS* 135). Ironically, Zeeny Vakil says 'I blame fiction' for the return of religious tensions: 'the followers of one fiction knock down another popular piece of make-believe, and bingo! It's war' (*MLS* 351). Moor himself, unable to make sense of the revelation that it was his own father who killed his mother – a revelation made immediately before Miranda's shooting of Uë – admits, 'I was lost in fictions, and murder was all around' (*MLS* 418). Moor has retained his truth claim to this point, almost like a fetish. 'I must peel off history, the prism of the past,' we find him saying one-third of the way through the novel. 'It is time for a sort of ending, for the truth about myself to struggle out from under my parents' stifling power' (*MLS* 136). Later, as he faces up to Uma's instability, he forces himself to realize: 'This is not a game. This is happening. It is my life, our life, and this its shape. This its true shape, the shape behind all shapes, the shape that reveals itself only at the moment of truth.' But later still there are still darker truths to acknowledge.

> But now I knew everything. No more benefits of doubts. Uma, my beloved traitor, you were ready to play the game to the end; to murder me and watch my death while hallucinogens blew your mind.... It must be the plain truth; everything about Uma and Aurora, Aurora and me, me and Uma Sarasvati, my witch. I would set it all down, and surrender myself to his sentence. (*MLS* 280, 321–2)

Even as he is 'writing for his life' at Miranda's direction – awaiting his captor's 'sentence' – his obsession with the truth of his narration invites us to look over the novelist's shoulder, responsible as he is for his character's act of writing. We are invited to review the novel we have been reading: 'On my little table in that death-cell young Abraham Zogoiby wooed his spice-heiress and aligned himself with love and beauty against the forces of ugliness and hate; and was that true, or was I putting Aoi's words into my father's thought-bubble?' Carmen da Gama is just 'a creature of my mind': as are all the characters, 'as they must be, having no means of being other than through my words' (*MLS* 425). We accompany the writer as he sails close to the wind of his intention, confiding in what he deferentially calls 'my omnipotent reader' his authorial uncertainties, and asking for our understanding (*MLS* 145).[14]

Miranda's accomplices the Ramirez sisters tell Moor, on his predestined arrival at Benengeli, 'You have come on a great pilgrimage....A son in search of his lost mother's treasures' (*MLS* 400). He never finds or, at least, never retrieves the lost painting; no more did Rushdie himself, in the actual family incident on which this episode is also based. But he does find the greater treasure of himself, as has been promised from the outset: 'the story which points to me. On the run, I have turned the world into my pirate map, complete with clues, leading X-marks-the-spottily to the treasure of myself' (*MLS* 3). Walter Benjamin observed, 'Not only a man's knowledge or wisdom, but above all his real life – and this is the stuff that stories are made of – first assumes transmissible form at the moment of his death.'[15] Moor writes his story at the point of Vasco Miranda's gun, and takes the pages, literally, to his grave: 'I have used the last of my strength to make this pilgrimage' (*MLS* 422–3). It is a pilgrimage that ends with a positive vision, with the promise of resurrection and renewed hope – addressed appropriately enough, we may feel, through its carefully chosen cross-cultural references, to Rushdie's expectant, worldwide audience.

> *The world is full of sleepers waiting for their moment of return: Arthur sleeps in Avalon, Barbarossa in his cave. Finn MacCool lies in the Irish hillsides and the Worm Ouroboros on the bed of the Sundering Sea. Australia's ancestors, the Wandjina, take their ease underground, and somewhere, in a tangle of thorns, a beauty in a glass coffin awaits a prince's kiss. See: here is my flask. I'll drink some wine; and then, like a latter-day Van Winkle, I'll lay me down upon this graven stone... and hope to awaken, renewed and joyful, into a better time.* (MLS 433–4)

8

Conclusion

This study began with an appeal to the rights and responsibilities of the imagination, and should also end there. In an article he wrote for the *Guardian* on 14 February 1997 (the eighth anniversary of the *fatwa*) Rushdie reminded us of the contestation for reality that lies at the heart of European civilization, conducted and recorded as it is through stories. From the Greek myths of the south via the Norse creation legends to the enabling fictions of the Enlightenment, our narratives represent an ongoing discussion, an argument, an accumulation of values. But these values are now under threat as Europe equivocates over the prerogative of the imagination.

> EU leaders pay lip-service to the great European ideals – free expression, human rights, the Enlightenment, the right to dissent, the importance of the separation of church and state. But when these ideals come up against the powerful banalities of what is called 'reality' – trade, money, guns, power – then it's freedom that takes a dive.

This essay recalls the imaginative motivation behind all Rushdie's fiction. What are the status, the value, the power of narrative, as against (or alongside) the other modes of discourse that compose our culture? We may well respect the interventions Rushdie has made, in newspapers and in journals such as *Index on Censorship* and elsewhere, in defence of free speech. These arguments reach beyond his own case, and indeed beyond the category of literary criticism. They are addressed to us as pragmatic political beings within our own lives, as people with opinions, values, and a vote. They function in the *fraternité* of citizenhood; and Rushdie is certainly entitled to remind us of our responsibilities in this direction, and to urge us to exercise them. But the engagement of fiction belongs to another order – to our imaginative conditioning rather than to our actual conditions, to what Shelley called 'the primary laws of our nature' rather than to the law of the land (or the laws of another land). And here Rushdie's accomplishment is both more perplexing and more profound, and of more enduring value. In everything he has written, from *Grimus* to *The Moor's Last Sigh*, Rushdie has explored on our behalf the hazards of being human, the limits of our human nature, as far as fiction can fathom it; and then beyond, into the intimations that lie beyond story itself in the very ground of our mental activity, among the archetypal prefigurings of being.

As Ayesha led her pilgrims to Mecca, through the waters of the Arabian Sea (was it to death, or resurrection?), we should perhaps regard Salman Rushdie himself as a pilgrim of the imagination, and read each of his novels as a stage in that pilgrimage. Flapping Eagle is a pilgrim through the levels of reality he encounters on Calf Island; Saleem Sinai leads the imaginative pilgrimage of the midnight children into modern India; Omar Khayyam Shakil is a peripheral pilgrim on the penitential journey of Pakistan. *The Satanic Verses* is an over-determined pilgrimage: from the vision of the founding of Islam to the literal pilgrimage of Ayesha, from the free-fall metamorphosis 'even unto death' of Gibreel Farishta to the painful process of personal change that has to be endured by Saladin Chamcha before he can return to life, everything in this novel confirms that the transformation of life can be achieved only through travail. In the same spirit, Haroun takes his father on the healing voyage to the spring of storytelling. Rushdie's short stories involve several pilgrims, from Columbus as pilgrim-in-waiting in Spain to modern migrants making (or failing to make) their difficult way in different corners of the world. And Moraes Zogoiby, as we have seen, makes the reverse pilgrimage to that of Columbus, in search of his mother – from the real corruption of modern India to the fabled possibilities of medieval Spain.

On one of the many instances where he has sought to defend his *Satanic Verses*, and to acknowledge the commitment of others to its defence, Rushdie wrote of the 'inner multiplicity, this crowd within' that is 'often very difficult for artists to bear, let alone explain'. For 'the creative process is not unlike the processes of free societies, which are by their very nature divided, plural, even quarrelsome'. And this inner debate is the essence of our humanity. 'Within every artist – perhaps within every human imagination – there exists, to paraphrase Blake, a marriage between Heaven and Hell.'[1] Rumour has it that Rushdie's next novel, to be called *The Ground Beneath her Feet*, will be a variation on the story of Orpheus, the mythical pilgrim from this world to the next, the supreme artist mediating between life and death. One could hardly imagine a more suitable hero to continue Rushdie's own pilgrimage into the forests and deserts, the cities and seas, the heaven and hell of the imagination.

Notes

CHAPTER 1.   INTRODUCTION

1. *Shelley's Prose*, ed. David Lee Clark (London: Fourth Estate, 1988), 282–3.
2. Jonathan Swift, *A Tale of a Tub*, sect. VIII; ed. A. C. Guthkelch and D. Nichol Smith (Oxford: Clarendon Press, 1958), 157; Samuel Johnson, *Rambler*, no. 125 (28 May 1751); S. T. Coleridge, 'Dejection: An Ode', *Selected Poetry and Prose*, ed. Stephen Potter (London: Nonesuch Press, 1962), 107.
3. Laurence Sterne, *Tristram Shandy*, vol. II, ch. ii; ed. Ian Campbell Ross (Oxford: Oxford University Press, 1983), 170. Emile Zola's relegation of the role of the imagination for the novelist is argued in his essay 'Le sens du réel', from *Le Roman expérimental* (Paris, 1880). A brief account will be found in my *Realism* (London: Methuen, 1970), 29–31.
4. See the account of Wilson Harris's work in Bill Ashcroft, Gareth Griffiths, and Helen Tiffin, *The Empire Writes Back: Theory and Practice in Post-Colonial Literatures* (London: Routledge, 1989), 34–6, 149–54; and extracts in Bill Ashcroft, Gareth Griffiths, and Helen Tiffin (eds.), *The Post-Colonial Studies Reader* (London: Routledge, 1995), 188, 200–1.
5. Wallace Stevens, *Opus Posthumous* (London: Faber, 1954), 177.
6. J. R. R. Tolkien, *Tree and Leaf* (London: Unwin Hyman, 1964), 36–7.
7. Virginia Woolf, *Collected Essays*, ed. Leonard Woolf (London: Chatto, 1966), i. 320.
8. Steven Connor, *The English Novel in History, 1950–1995* (London: Macmillan, 1996), 31.
9. Ashcroft *et al.* (eds.), *The Post-Colonial Studies Reader*, 209.
10. The phrase was coined (or adopted) in an editorial from *The Crane Bag* reprinted in Mark Hederman and Richard Kearney (eds.), *The Crane Bag Book of Irish Studies* (Dublin: Blackwater Press, 1982). See David Cairns and Shaun Richards, *Writing Ireland* (Manchester: Manchester University Press, 1988), 149.
11. Benedict Anderson, *Imagined Communities: Reflections on the Origin and Spread of Nationalism* (London: Verso, 1991). Rushdie makes generous acknowledgement in his essays to the importance of Anderson's book

to his own thinking; it contains, he says, 'important stuff for the novelist' (*IH* 382).

12. *Shelley's Prose*, 279.

13. Lisa Appignanesi and Sara Maitland (eds.), *The Rushdie File* (London: ICA/ Fourth Estate, 1989), 181, 142.

14. *For Rushdie: Essays by Arab and Muslim Writers in Defense of Free Speech* (New York: George Braziller, 1994), 261.

15. Ziauddin Sardar and Meryl Wyn Davies, *Distorted Imagination: Lessons from the Rushdie Affair* (London: Grey Seal, 1990). Sardar writes: '[Rushdie's] perspective as it unfolds through the entire course of his writing is best described as an angle of attack formed by the Orientalist view of Islam' (p. 127).

16. Richard Webster, *A Brief History of Blasphemy: Liberalism, Censorship, and 'The Satanic Verses'* (Southwold: Orwell, 1990), 148.

17. D. J. Enright, 'The Old Man Comes to his Senses', *Selected Poems* (London: Chatto, 1968), 33.

18. Connor, *The English Novel in History*, 33. See also the assessment by Andrzej Gasiorek in *Post-War British Fiction: Realism and After* (London: Arnold, 1995), 167.

19. D. H. Lawrence, 'The Novel', in Bruce Steele (ed.), *Study of Thomas Hardy and Other Essays* (Cambridge: Cambridge University Press, 1985), 155.

20. S. T. Coleridge, *Biographia Literaria*, ch. 14; ed. George Watson (London Dent, 1965), 174.

21. See the articles on *Midnight's Children* by Keith Wilson, Nancy E. Batty, and Patricia Merivale in M. D. Fletcher (ed.), *Reading Rushdie: Perspectives on the Fiction of Salman Rushdie* (Amsterdam: Rodopi, 1994), and also the further references in the section on the novel in the Annotated Bibliography (pp. 362–71). See also Walter Göbel and Damian Grant, 'Salman Rushdie's Silver Medal', in David Pierce and Peter de Voogd (eds.), *Laurence Sterne in Modernism and Postmodernism* (Amsterdam: Rodopi, 1996), 87–98.

22. Laurence Sterne, *Tristram Shandy*, vol. I, ch. xxii, ed. Ross, p. 58.

23. Una Chaudhuri, 'Imaginative Maps: Excerpts from a Conversation with Salman Rushdie', *Turnstile*, 2/1 (1990), 36–47. The text of this interview may be accessed at website http://www.crl.com/~subir/rushdie/uc_maps.html.

24. 'Salman Rushdie talks to Alastair Niven', *Wasafiri*, 26 (1997), 55.

25. Timothy Brennan, *Salman Rushdie and the Third World: Myths of the Nation* (London: Macmillan, 1989), 30–1. Brennan's book also takes up Benedict Anderson's idea of the novel as being, along with the newspaper, a crucial ingredient in the formation of the 'imagined community'.

26. Ibid. 34, 69.

27. Ibid. 134.
28. Milan Kundera, *Testaments Betrayed* (London: Faber, 1995), 26.
29. Brennan, *Salman Rushdie and the Third World*, 135, 49.
30. Aijaz Ahmad, *In Theory: Classes, Nations, Literatures* (London: Verso, 1992), 128.
31. Ibid. 131, 134.
32. Ibid. 149–50, 135.
33. Oscar Wilde, 'The Truth of Masks', in *Intentions* and *The Soul of Man* (London: Methuen, 1969), 269.
34. Brennan, *Salman Rushdie and the Third World*, 43.
35. Ahmad, *In Theory*, 154–5, 134, 141.
36. Tim Parnell, 'Salman Rushdie: From Colonial Politics to Postmodern Politics', in Bart Moore-Gilbert (ed.), *Writing India 1757–1900: The Literature of British India* (Manchester: Manchester University Press, 1996), 254–7.
37. James Harrison, *Salman Rushdie* (New York: Twayne, 1992), 128.
38. Fletcher (ed.), *Reading Rushdie*, 66.
39. Malise Ruthven, *A Satanic Affair: Salman Rushdie and the Wrath of Islam* (London: Chatto, 1991), 13. (First published as *A Satanic Affair: Salman Rushdie and the Rage of Islam* (1990).)
40. Ibid. 15–18.
41. Michael Gorra, *After Empire: Scott, Naipaul, Rushdie* (Chicago: Chicago University Press, 1997), 127.
42. Kundera, *Testaments Betrayed*, 26.
43. See the Appendix on 'The Rushdie Affair', pp. 88–93.
44. *For Rushdie*, 6, 10.
45. Sadik Al-Azm, 'The Importance of Being Earnest about Salman Rushdie', in Fletcher (ed.), *Reading Rushdie*, 258–77.
46. Srinivias Aravamudan, 'Being God's Postman is no Fun, Yaar', in Fletcher (ed.), *Reading Rushdie*, 197–8.
47. Stephanie Newell, 'The Other God: Salman Rushdie's "New" Aesthetic', *Literature and History*, 3rd ser., 1/2 (1992), 67–87.
48. Catherine Cundy, *Salman Rushdie* (Manchester: Manchester University Press, 1997), 22, 37, 52–3.
49. Ibid. 55. For Cundy's consideration of this aspect in the later novels, see ibid. 78–9, 116.
50. Inderpal Grewal, 'Salman Rushdie: Marginality, Women, and *Shame*', in Fletcher (ed.), *Reading Rushdie*, 123–4, 143.
51. Anuradha Dingwaney Needham, 'The Politics of Post-Colonial Identity in Salman Rushdie', in Fletcher (ed.), *Reading Rushdie*, 149, 153, 157.
52. M. D. Fletcher, 'Introduction', in Fletcher (ed.), *Reading Rushdie*, 1–20. Likewise, Fletcher's own essay, 'Rushdie's *Shame* as Apologue' (pp. 97–108), proposes this unfamiliar formal category (supplemented with

ridicule, satire, farce, and fairy tale), which is unlikely to inspire the reader.

53. Ib Johansen, 'The Flight from the Enchanter: Reflections on Salman Rushdie's *Grimus*', in ibid. 25; Catherine Cundy, ' "Rehearsing Voices": Salman Rushdie's *Grimus*', in ibid. 48.

54. Peter Brigg, 'Salman Rushdie's Novels: The Disorder in Fantastic Order', in ibid. 181.

55. These descriptions are taken from the section on *The Satanic Verses* in the Annotated Bibliography in ibid. 381–95.

56. Uma Parameswaran, 'New Dimensions Courtesy of the Whirling Demons: Word-Play in *Grimus*', in ibid. 42; Keith Wilson, '*Midnight's Children* and Reader Responsibility', in ibid. 62; Patricia Merivale, 'Saleem Fathered by Oscar: Intertextual Strategies in *Midnight's Children* and *The Tin Drum*', in ibid. 84, 94.

57. See Aravamudan, 'Being God's Postman'; Kundera, *Testaments Betrayed*; and Feroza Jussawalla, 'Rushdie's *Dastan-e-Dilruba: The Satanic Verses* as Rushdie's Love Letter to Islam', *Diacritics*, 26 (1996), 50–73.

58. See Nancy E. Batty, 'The Art of Suspense: Rushdie's 1001 (Mid-)-Nights,' in Fletcher (ed.), *Reading Rushdie*, 69–82; Connor, *The English Novel in History*, 30–3, 112–27; Michael M. Fischer and Mehdi Abedi, 'Bombay Talkies, the Word and the World: Salman Rushdie's *Satanic Verses*', *Cultural Anthropology*, 5/2 (1990), 107–59; N. Rombes Jr., '*The Satanic Verses* as Cinematic Narrative', *Literature/Film Quarterly*, 11/1 (1993), 47–53.

59. Ashis Nandy, *The Intimate Enemy: Loss and Recovery of Self under Colonialism* (New Delhi: Oxford University Press, 1983), pp. xvii–xviii.

60. 'Salman Rushdie Talks to Alastair Niven', *Wasafiri*, 26 (1997), 53.

61. A selection from the essays in *Imaginary Homelands*: Rushdie praises Rudyard Kipling's 'invented Indiaspeak', and the 'demotic voice of black Afrikaner South Africa' in Rian Malan (*IH* 77, 198); he notes Gunther Grass's contribution to the reconstruction of the German language after the war, and the way Gabriel Marquez's grandmother functioned as a 'linguistic lodestone' for him (*IH* 279, 300); he appreciates E. L. Doctorow's 'great rush of language', and Thomas Pynchon's 'brilliant way with names' (*IH* 300, 355). At the same time, he deplores the 'rotten writing' of Benazir Bhutto's autobiography, and regrets the 'dead language' of *Handsworth Songs* (*IH* 57, 115). Even Kurt Vonnegut fails in this respect, with *Hocus Pocus*; in this novel, 'that old hocus-pocus, language, just isn't working' (*IH* 360).

62. Salman Rushdie and Elizabeth West (eds.), *The Vintage Book of Indian Writing 1947–1997* (London: Vintage, 1997), p. xviii.

63. Rustom Bharucha, 'Rushdie's Whale', in Fletcher (ed.), *Reading Rushdie*, 162, 165, 169–70.

64 Jacqueline Bardolph, 'Language is Courage', in ibid. 212.

65. Harrison, *Salman Rushdie*, 127. See also the appreciation of Rushdie's language in the Introduction by Anita Desai to the Everyman edition of *Midnight's Children* (1995), pp. ix–x, xviii-xix.

CHAPTER 2. *GRIMUS*

1. Rushdie himself recalls, 'I had one novel rejected, [and] abandoned two others' before *Grimus* (*IH* 1). According to Ian Hamilton, there was an early novel about Rugby called 'Terminal Report', and also (after *Grimus*) another Indian novel with more political edge, called 'Madame Rama', which was 'plundered' for *Midnight's Children* ('The First Life of Salman Rushdie', *New Yorker*, 71/42 (25 Dec. 1995), 96, 100, 102).

2. Henry Fielding, *Tom Jones*, bk. II, ch. 1; ed. R. P. Mutter (Harmondsworth: Penguin, 1966), 88.

3. James Joyce, *A Portrait of the Artist as a Young Man* (Harmondsworth: Penguin, 1968), 253. One of the characters in *The Moor's Last Sigh* elaborates a social philosophy based upon Joyce's phrase, which he has supposedly picked up from the serial publication of the novel in *The Egoist*; and which he attempts to promulgate in a paper called *Towards a Provisional Theory of the Transformational Fields of Conscience* (*MLS* 20).

4. Timothy Brennan, *Salman Rushdie and the Third World: Myths of the Nation* (London: Macmillan, 1989), 70.

5. Liz Calder's original assessment is worth recalling here: 'although it was barmy in some ways, all over the place, I thought it was amazing,' she says, particularly for its 'extraordinary use of language' (Hamilton, 'The First Life of Salman Rushdie', 101).

6. Lisa Appignanesi and Sara Maitland (eds.), *The Rushdie File* (London: ICA/Fourth Estate, 1989), 30.

7. Brennan, *Salman Rushdie and the Third World*, 72, 74; Catherine Cundy, *Salman Rushdie* (Manchester: Manchester University Press, 1997), 16.

CHAPTER 3. *MIDNIGHT'S CHILDREN*

1. See John Haffenden, *Novelists in Interview* (London: Methuen, 1985), 237–8.

2. See Charu Verma, 'Padma's Tragedy: A Feminist Deconstruction of Rushdie's *Midnight's Children*', in Sushila Singh (ed.), *Feminism and Recent Fiction in English* (New Delhi: Prestige, 1991), 154–62.

3. Laurence Sterne, *Tristram Shandy*, vol. II, ch. xi; ed. Ian Campbell Ross

(Oxford: Oxford University Press, 1983), 87.

4. Published in the original Spanish as *Rayuela* in 1963; translated as *Hopscotch* in 1966.

5. Timothy Brennan, *Salman Rushdie and the Third World: Myths of the Nation* (London: Macmillan, 1989), 85.

6. Andrzej Gasiorek, *Post-War British Fiction: Realism and After* (London: Arnold, 1995), 167.

7. Keith Wilson, '*Midnight's Children* and Reader Responsibility', in M. D. Fletcher (ed.), *Reading Rushdie: Perspectives on the Fiction of Salman Rushdie* (Amsterdam: Rodopi, 1994), 55–68.

8. *The Tempest*, I. ii. 49.

9. Sir Philip Sidney, *An Apology for Poetry*, ed. Geoffrey Shepherd (Manchester: Manchester University Press, 1973), 123.

10. Wordsworth and Coleridge, *Lyrical Ballads*, ed. Derek Roper (London: Collins, 1968), 33.

11. See e.g. Philip Engblom, 'A Multitude of Voices: Carnivalization and Dialogicality in the Novels of Salman Rushdie', in Fletcher (ed.), *Reading Rushdie*, 293–304.

12. Published in 1904 and 1902 respectively. Both stories appear in Kipling's *Mrs Bathurst and Other Stories* (Oxford: Oxford University Press, 1991).

13. See the interview with Steve Crawshaw in the *Independent on Sunday*, 8 Feb. 1998, pp. 29–31.

14. Brennan, *Salman Rushdie and the Third World*, 38, 69, 140, 159.

15. Steven Connor, *The English Novel in History, 1950–1995* (London: Macmillan, 1996), 31–2.

16. See e.g. Patricia Merivale, 'Saleem Fathered by Oscar: Intertextual Strategies in *Midnight's Children* and *The Tin Drum*', in Fletcher (ed.), *Reading Rushdie*, 83–96.

17. Daniel Defoe, *Robinson Crusoe*, ed. J. Donald Crowley (Oxford: Oxford University Press, 1972), 45.

18. See the article by Clement Hawes, 'Leading History by the Nose: The Turn to the Eighteenth Century in *Midnight's Children*', *Modern Fiction Studies*, 39/1 (1993), 147–68. Hawes argues that the 'logic of the baby-swap is precisely against the grain of conventional "birth mysteries"', which, elsewhere, were used to authorize essentialist and ultimately racist attitudes.

19. Haffenden, *Novelists in Interview*, 239.

20. Joseph Conrad, *Heart of Darkness*, ed. Paul O'Prey (Harmondsworth: Penguin, 1983), 66; J. G. Ballard, *The Drowned World* (London: Berkley, 1962). There may also be a recollection here of Angela Carter's story 'Master', from her 1974 collection *Fireworks*.

CHAPTER 4. *SHAME*

1. See Ian Hamilton, 'The First Life of Salman Rushdie', *New Yorker*, 71/42 (25 Dec. 1995), 105 ('This Booker night of "Shame" has now passed into legend, by means of a Rushdiesque process of telling and retelling').
2. Timothy Brennan, *Salman Rushdie and the Third World: Myths of the Nation* (London: Macmillan, 1989), 123; Aijaz Ahmad, *In Theory: Classes, Nations, Literatures* (London: Verso, 1992), 139; Catherine Cundy, *Salman Rushdie* (Manchester: Manchester University Press, 1997), 44.
3. Malise Ruthven, *A Satanic Affair: Salman Rushdie and the Wrath of Islam* (London: Chatto, 1991), 14; James Harrison, *Salman Rushdie* (New York: Twayne, 1992), 24; Keith Booker, 'Beauty and the Beast: Dualism as Despotism in the fiction of Salman Rushdie', in M. D. Fletcher (ed.), *Reading Rushdie: Perspectives in the fiction of Salman Rushdie* (Amsterdam: Rodopi, 1994), 249.
4. John Haffenden, *Novelists in Interview* (London: Methuen, 1985), 240–3.
5. Ibid. 237.
6. See e.g. Ashutosh Banerjee, 'A Critical Study of *Shame*', and Suresh Chandra, 'The Metaphor of Shame: Rushdie's Fact-Fiction'. Both these articles, originally published in the *Commonwealth Review*, are reprinted in G. R. Taneja and R.K. Dhawan (eds.), *The Novels of Salman Rushdie* (New Delhi: Prestige, 1992).
7. Homi Bhabha, 'Unpacking my Library... Again', in Iain Chambers and Linda Curti (eds.), *The Post-Colonial Question* (London: Routledge, 1996), 208.
8. Jane Austen, *Mansfield Park*, ch. 15; ed. Kathryn Sutherland (Harmondsworth: Penguin, 1996), 122.
9. Timothy Brennan, '*Shame*'s Holy Book', in Fletcher (ed.), *Reading Rushdie*, 112.
10. Rushdie comments: 'The book is partly about the way in which women are socially repressed....Omar Khayyam's mothers are another instance of female solidarity, which is really brought about by the way in which they are obliged to live in the male-dominated society' (Haffenden, *Novelists in Interview*), 256.
11. Salman Rushdie, '*Midnight's Children* and *Shame*', *Kunapipi* 7/1 (1985), 13.
12. Jonathan Swift, *Gulliver's Travels*, vol. IV, ch. viii; ed. Paul Turner (Oxford: Oxford University Press, 1971), 270. For the reference to *A Tale of a Tub*, see Ch. 7, n. 11 below.
13. Henry James, *The Art of the Novel* (New York: Charles Scribner's Sons, 1934), 231.

14. Timothy Brennan, '*Shame*'s Holy Book', in Fletcher (ed.), *Reading Rushdie*, 119.
15. Haffenden, *Novelists in Interview*, 254–5.

CHAPTER 5. *THE SATANIC VERSES*

1. See especially Malise Ruthven, *A Satanic Affair: Salman Rushdie and the Wrath of Islam* (London: Chatto, 1991), ch. 1, and Milan Kundera, 'The Day Panurge No Longer Makes People Laugh', in *Testaments Betrayed* (London: Faber, 1995), 1–33. Also the contributions by D. J. Enright, Homi Bhabha, Naguib Mahfouz, Carlos Fuentes, Michael Ignatieff, and others to Lisa Appignanesi and Sara Maitland (eds.), *The Rushdie File* (London: ICA/Fourth Estate, 1989); and the general tenor of contributions to *For Rushdie: Essays by Arab and Muslim Writers in Defense of Free Speech* (New York: George Braziller, 1994).
2. Appignanesi and Maitland (eds.), *The Rushdie File*, 6–7.
3. See Pierre François, 'Salman Rushdie's Philosophical Materialism in *The Satanic Verses*', in M. D. Fletcher (ed.), *Reading Rushdie: Perspectives on the Fiction of Salman Rushdie* (Amsterdam: Rodopi, 1994), 305–20, at 305. Milan Kundera also has interesting observations on how the structure of the novel serves its meaning, in *Testaments Betrayed*, 21–3.
4. *Hamlet*, II. ii. 594–5.
5. Steven Connor, *The English Novel in History, 1950–1995* (London: Macmillan, 1996), 124.
6. For a further consideration of this question, see Walter Göbel and Damian Grant, 'Salman Rushdie's Silver Medal', in David Pierce and Peter de Voogd (eds.), *Laurence Sterne in Modernism and Postmodernism* (Amsterdam: Rodopi, 1996), 87–98.
7. See Ruthven, *A Satanic Affair*, 24–5.
8. Walter Benjamin proposes that 'memory is the epic faculty *par excellence*' (*Illuminations* (London: Fontana, 1973), 96).
9. Connor, *The English Novel in History*, 113.
10. Srinivas Aravamudan, 'Being God's Postman is no Fun, Yaar', in Fletcher (ed.), *Reading Rushdie*, 187–208.
11. Ibid. 199–203. Aravamudan notes: 'The precise linguistic, indeed palindromic, opposite of *muhammad* "the glorified" or "the praised" in Arabic, is *mudhammam*, meaning "reprobate" or "apostate"' (p. 202).
12. Samuel Beckett, *Company* (London: Faber, 1980), 30.
13. Fawzia Afzal-Khan, *Cultural Imperialism and the Indo-English Novel* (Pennsylvania: Penn State University Press, 1993), 168–9. See also Feroza Jussawalla, 'Rushdie's *Dastan-e-Dilruba: The Satanic Verses* as Rushdie's Love-Letter to Islam', *Diacritics*, 26 (1996), 50–73.
14. In an author's note to a leaflet published by The Book Trust in

conjunction with the British Council in 1987, Rushdie remarks: 'First the writer invents the books; then, perhaps, the books invent the writer.'

15. Steve McDonogh (ed.), *The Rushdie Letters: Freedom to Speak, Freedom to Write* (Dingle, Co. Derry: Brandon, 1993), 125–83. All facts and quotations in the next three paragraphs are taken from this source.

16. Rushdie's own account of this episode may be found in the essay 'One Thousand Days in a Balloon' (*IH* 434–7).

17. James Joyce, *A Portrait of the Artist as a Young Man* (Harmondsworth: Penguin, 1960), 203.

18. Simon Lee, *The Cost of Free Speech* (London: Faber, 1990), 88.

19. *The Rushdie Letters*, 141.

20. Richard Webster, *A Brief History of Blasphemy: Liberalism, Censorship, and 'The Satanic Verses'* (Southwold: Orwell, 1990).

21. Lee, *The Cost of Free Speech*, 103.

22. See, for a detailed study of this aspect, Joel Kuortti, *Place of the Sacred: The Rhetoric of the* Satanic Verses *Affair* (Frankfurt: Peter Lang, 1997).

23. Ruthven, *A Satanic Affair*, 48.

24. Ibid. 47.

25. Lee, *The Cost of Free Speech*, 47.

26. In an interview published in 1996, Rushdie welcomed the fact that *The Satanic Verses* 'is gradually getting off the news pages and getting back into the world of books' (Colin McCabe *et al.*, 'Salman Rushdie Talks to the London Consortium about *The Satanic Verses*', *Critical Quarterly*, 38/2 (1996), 66). This process should now be accelerated.

CHAPTER 6.   *HAROUN AND THE SEA OF STORIES* AND *EAST, WEST*

1. James Fenton,' Keeping Up with Salman Rushdie', *New York Review of Books*, 28 Mar. 1991, p. 31.

2. Several of the critical articles on *Haroun* draw parallels with Rushdie's personal situation. See the relevant entries in the Annotated Bibliography in M. D. Fletcher (ed.), *Reading Rushdie: Perspectives on the Fiction of Salman Rushdie* (Amsterdam: Rodopi, 1994), 395–6.

3. In Jorge Luis Borges, *Labyrinths* (Harmondsworth: Penguin, 1970).

4. One critic suggests that Rushdie's smuggling in of this female narrator is a gesture of solidarity with the woman novelist: see Marlene S. Barr '*Haroun* and Seeing Women's Stories: Salman Rushdie and Marianne Wiggins', in Barr (ed.), *Lost in Space: Probing Feminist Science Fiction and Beyond* (Chapel Hill, NC: University of North Carolina Press, 1993).

5. Jonathan Swift, *A Tale of a Tub*, sect. VIII; ed. A. C. Guthkelch and

D. Nichol Smith (Oxford: Clarendon Press, 1958), 158.

6. There is probably a reference in both these instances to Lewis Carroll's use of the chessboard to represent regulation in the *Alice* stories.

7. Rushdie has remarked that it was when he realized there was a story to be made of the stories, which taken together represent 'a step by step journey', that he decided to 'put them together in a book': 'Salman Rushdie Talks to Alastair Niven', *Wasafiri*, 26 (1997), 54. Catherine Cundy has actually suggested that the interlocking of the stories is intended to produce a parallel to the *Mahabharata*; but, although she cites what she sees as specific allusions (as where the unwinding of the ayah's sari by the escalator in 'The Courter' parallels the disrobing of Drapaudi), the idea of a systematic counterpoint seems implausible (*Salman Rushdie* (Manchester: Manchester University Press, 1997), 3–4).

8. It is possible that Rushdie took the idea of a congregation of fictional characters from Christine Brooke-Rose's novel *Textermination* (Manchester: Carcanet, 1991). In this intriguing work, hundreds of characters from fiction, film, and television attend a conference in San Francisco to 'compete for being' in the world of their readers and viewers. If so, it is only a compliment returned, since among the characters convoked by Brooke-Rose is Gibreel Farishta himself, from *The Satanic Verses*.

9. Walter Benjamin, 'The Storyteller', in *Illuminations* (London: Fontana, 1973), 93.

10. 'Salman Rushdie talks to Alastair Niven', 54.

CHAPTER 7. *THE MOOR'S LAST SIGH*

1. See e.g. the reviews by Peter Kemp (*Sunday Times*, 3 Sept. 1995), Michael Wood (*London Review of Books*, 7 Sept. 1995), Orhan Pamuk (*TLS*, 8 Sept. 1995), James Wood (*Guardian*, 8 Sept, 1995), J. M. Coetzee (*New York Review of Books*, 21 Mar. 1996).

2. Catherine Cundy, *Salman Rushdie* (Manchester: Manchester University Press, 1997), 116, 110.

3. J. M. Coetzee, *New York Review of Books*, 21 Mar. 1996, p. 14.

4. There may well be an allusion here to Adrian Mitchell's lines on Charlie Parker: 'He breathed in air, he breathed out light / Charlie Parker was my delight' ('Goodbye', *For Beauty Douglas* (Alison & Busby, 1982). Especially when the next phrase reads: '– *We breathe light* – the trees pipe up.'

5. Henry James, *The Art of the Novel* (New York: Charles Scribner's Sons, 1934), 313.

6. Samuel Beckett, *Molloy: Malone Dies: The Unnamable* (London: John

Calder, 1959), 7.

7. '*Midnight's Children* had history as a scaffolding on which to hang the book; this one [*The Satanic Verses*] doesn't' (Rushdie in interview with Sean French, in Lisa Appignanesi and Sara Maitland (eds.), *The Rushdie File* (London: ICA/Fourth Estate, 1989), 8).

8. The personal feeling may be authorized by the fact that the novel with its palimpsest metaphor relates to a Rushdie family anecdote concerning an actual portrait of his mother, lost in all probability through being overpainted (see 13 below).

9. Orhan Pamuk remarks on the danger (just avoided here) of lapsing into an 'old-style Indian melodrama', and suggests that the 'over-abundance of fame, money, sex, and glamour gives the book an aura of a grotesque jet-set novel set in Bombay' (*TLS*, 8 Sept. 1995, p. 3).

10. *Shelley's Prose*, ed. David Lee Clark (London: Fourth Estate, 1988), 283.

11. 'Last Week I saw a Woman *flay'd*, and you will hardly believe, how much it altered her Person for the worse' (Jonathan Swift, *A Tale of a Tub*, sect. IX; ed. A. C. Guthkelch and D. Nichol Smith (Oxford: Clarendon Press, 1958), 173; Beckett, *Molloy: Malone Dies: The Unnamable*, 268–9.

12. John Keats, letter to George and Thomas Keats, 21 Dec. 1817, in *Letters of John Keats*, ed. Frederick Page (London: Oxford University Press, 1954), 53.

13. This anecdote from Rushdie's family was explored in the programme, 'The Lost Portrait' (transmitted by BBC 2 on 11 Sept. 1995), describing Rushdie's visit to India in search of a portrait of his mother. Rushdie found the artist, but the canvas had been reused and the painting was therefore untraceable.

14. J. M. Coetzee is, however, not impressed by this gesture, which he describes as part of a 'postmodern textual romp'. As he sees it, there is a ready solution to the Moor's problem: 'If as self-narrator he wants to escape the inessential determinants of his life, he need only storytell his way out of them' (*New York Review of Books*, 21 Mar. 1996, p. 15).

15. Walter Benjamin, 'The Storyteller', in *Illuminations* (London: Fontana, 1973), 94.

CONCLUSION

1. In Steve MacDonogh (ed.) in association with Article 19, *The Rushdie Letters: Freedom to Speak, Freedom to Write* (Dingle, Co. Derry: Brandon, 1993), 123.

Select Bibliography

WORKS BY SALMAN RUSHDIE

Novels
Grimus (London: Victor Gollancz, 1975; Grafton, 1977).
Midnight's Children (London: Jonathan Cape, 1981; Picador, 1983; Everyman's Library, 1995, with an introduction by Anita Desai).
Shame (London: Jonathan Cape, 1983; Picador, 1984).
The Satanic Verses (London: Viking, 1988; Delaware: The Consortium, 1992).
The Moor's Last Sigh (London: Jonathan Cape, 1995).

Short Stories
East, West (London: Jonathan Cape, 1994).

Children's Stories
Haroun and the Sea of Stories (London: Granta Books/Penguin, 1990).

Poems
'6 March 1989', *Granta*, 28 (Aug. 1989), 28–9.
'Crusoe', *Granta* 31 (Sept. 1990), 128.

Film and Television
'The Painter and the Pest', (Channel 4, 2 Dec. 1985; text in *Imaginary Homelands*, 152–6).
'The Riddle of Midnight: India, August 1987' (Channel 4, 27 Mar. 1988: text in *Imaginary Homelands*, 26–33).
'The Lost Portrait' (BBC 2, 11 Sept. 1995).

Non-Fiction
The Jaguar Smile: A Nicaraguan Journey (London: Viking, 1987; Picador, 1987).

Imaginary Homelands: Essays and Criticism 1981–1991 (London: Granta Books, 1991).

The Wizard of Oz: A Short Text about Magic (BFI Film Classics; London: BFI, 1992).

Introduction to Rudyard Kipling, *Soldiers Three* and *In Black and White* (Harmondsworth: Penguin, 1993), p. ix–xv.

Introduction to Angela Carter, *Burning Your Boats: Collected Short Stories* (London: Vintage, 1996), pp. ix–xiv.

Edited (with Elizabeth West), *The Vintage Book of Indian Writing 1947–97* (London: Vintage, 1997); Introduction by Rushdie, pp. ix–xxii.

SELECTED INTERVIEWS

Over 70 interviews are listed in Joel Kuortti, *The Salman Rushdie Bibliography* (Frankfurt: Peter Lang, 1997), between May 1981 and April 1996; in books, journals, newspapers, and on video. Some of the more substantial interviews are listed here, in chronological order.

Durix, Jean Pierre, 'Interview with Salman Rushdie', *Kunapipi*, 4/2 (1982), 17–26.

Haffenden, John, 'An Interview with Salman Rushdie', *Literary Review* (Sept. 1983, 26–31; repr. as 'Salman Rushdie', in John Haffenden (ed.), *Novelists in Interview* (London: Methuen, 1985), 231–61.

Dharker, Rani, 'An Interview with Salman Rushdie', *New Quest*, 42 (1983), 351–60.

Brooks, David, 'Interview with Salman Rushdie', *Helix*, 19–20 (1984/5), 55–69.

Craven, Peter, 'Interview', *Scripsi*, 3/2–3 (1985), 107–26.

Lawson, Mark, 'Fishing for Salman', *Independent* (Magazine; 10 Sept. 1988), 58–62.

Jain, Mahdu, 'My Theme is Fanaticism', *India Today* (New Delhi; 15 Sept. 1988).

Mason, Roger Burford, 'Salman Rushdie', *PN Review* (Manchester), 15/4, (no. 66, 1989), 15–19.

Chaudhuri, Una, 'Imaginative Maps', *Turnstile*, (2/1 (1990), 36–47.

Morrison, Blake, 'An Interview with Salman Rushdie', *Granta*, 31 (Spring 1990), 113–25.

Fenton, James, 'Keeping Up with Salman Rushdie', *New York Review of Books* 38/6 (28 Mar. 1991), 24–32.

'Salman Rushdie Speaks to English PEN', *PEN International*, 42/1 (1992), 3–8.

Rushdie, Salman, 'An Interview with Toni Morrison', *Brick*, 44 (1992), 33–9.

Banville, John, 'An Interview with Salman Rushdie', *New York Review of Books*, 40/5 (4 Mar. 1993), 34–6.

Cronenberg, David, 'Goodfellas', *Shift* 3/4 (July–Aug. 1995), 20–7.

MacCabe, Colin, *et al.*, 'Salman Rushdie Talks to the London Consortium about *The Satanic Verses*', *Critical Quarterly*, 38/2 (1996), 51–70.

'Salman Rushdie Talks to Alastair Niven', *Wasafiri*, 26 (1997), 52–7.

BIBLIOGRAPHY

Kuortti, Joel, *The Salman Rushdie Bibliography* (Frankfurt: Peter Lang, 1997).

See also the bibliographical Appendix (353–9) and Annotated Bibliography (361–96) in M. D. Fletcher (ed.), *Reading Rushdie* (Amsterdam: Rodopi, 1994).

BIOGRAPHY

Hamilton, Ian, 'The First Life of Salman Rushdie', *New Yorker*, 71/42 (25 Dec. 1995), 90–113. Repr. in Ian Hamilton, *The Trouble with Money and Other Essays* (London: Bloomsbury, 1998). This biographical essay draws on many personal and published sources, not least from Rushdie himself. Hamilton acknowledges Rushdie's 'generous help' with the essay, which was given on one condition: 'provided that I did not pursue my researches beyond what was for him the final day of his first life: Valentine's Day, 1989.'

Weatherby, William J., *Salman Rushdie: Sentenced to Death* (New York: Carroll & Graf, 1990).

CRITICAL STUDIES

Books on Rushdie

Brennan, Timothy, *Salman Rushdie and the Third World: Myths of the Nation* (London: Macmillan, 1989). A sustained critique of Rushdie's ideological position, working through an analysis of the novels from *Grimus* to *The Satanic Verses*.

Cundy, Catherine, *Salman Rushdie* (Manchester: Manchester University Press, 1997). A novel-by-novel account of Rushdie's fiction, including a 'Postscript' on *The Moor's Last Sigh*, with emphasis on contexts and intertexts; the feminist perspective finds unfavourably for the author.

Fletcher, M. D. (ed.), *Reading Rushdie: Perspectives on the Fiction of Salman Rushdie* (Amsterdam: Rodopi, 1994). The most useful critical work to date: a collection of twenty-two essays from different sources, focusing on each of the novels in turn. Contains a very useful Annotated Bibliography and 'Some Books and Articles about the Rushdie Affair'.

Goonetilleke, D. C. R. A., *Salman Rushdie* (London: Macmillan, 1998). A loosely structured commentary on the novels, linking them to Rushdie's biography.

Harrison, James, *Salman Rushdie* (New York: Twayne, 1992). Considers each of the novels (to *The Satanic Verses*) in the context of Rushdie's complex background and influence; corrective to some postcolonial theory.

Parameswaran, Uma, *The Perforated Sheet: Essays on Salman Rushdie's Art* (New Delhi: Affiliated, 1988). A collection of seven previously published articles.

Petersson, Margareta, *Unending Metamorphoses: Myth, Satire, and Religion in Salman Rushdie's Novels* (Lund, Sweden: Lund University Press, 1996). Not seen.

Rao, M. Madhusan, *Salman Rushdie's Fiction: A Study:* The Satanic Verses *Excluded* (New Delhi: Sterling, 1992). A study of the relation between 'timelessness' and history in Rushdie's first three novels.

Seminck, Hans, *A Novel Visible but Unseen: A Thematic Analysis of Salman Rushdie's 'The Satanic Verses'* (Gent: Studia Germanica Gandensia, 1993). Not seen.

Taneja, G. R., and Dhawan, R. K. (eds.), *The Novels of Salman Rushdie* (New Delhi: Prestige, 1992). A collection of twenty-four essays mainly by Indian writers, previously published in the *Journal for Commonwealth Studies*. Grouped around the novels, the essays, and 'Themes and Techniques.'

Books with chapters, sections, or essays on Rushdie

Acheson, James (ed.), *The British and Irish Novel since 1960* (Houndmills: Macmillan, 1991).

Adam, Ian, and Tiffin, Helen (eds.), *Past the Last Post: Theorizing Post-Colonialism and Postmodernism* (New York: Harvester, 1991).

Afzal-Khan, Fawzia, *Cultural Imperialism and the Indo-English Novel: Genre and Ideology in the Novels of R. K. Narayan, Anita Desai, Kamala Markandaya, and Salman Rushdie* (Pennsylvania: Pennsylvania State University Press, 1993).

Ahmad, Aijaz, *In Theory: Classes, Nations, Literatures* (London: Verso, 1992).

Alexander, Maguerite, *Flights from Realism: Themes and Strategies in*

Postmodernist British and American Fiction (London: Arnold, 1990).

Ashcroft, Bill, Griffiths, Gareth, and Tiffin, Helen, *The Empire Writes Back: Theory and Practice in Post-Colonial Literatures* (London: Routledge, 1989).

Ashcroft, Bill, Griffiths, Gareth, and Tiffin, Helen, (eds.), *The Post-Colonial Studies Reader* (London: Routledge, 1995).

Becker, Carol, *The Subversive Imagination: Artists, Society, and Responsibility* (New York: Routledge, 1994).

Benson, Eugene, and Conolly, L. W. (eds.), *Encyclopaedia of Post-Colonial Literatures in English* (London: Routledge, 1994).

Bertens, Hans, *The Idea of the Postmodern: A History* (London: Routledge, 1995).

Bevan, David, *Literature and Exile* (Amsterdam: Rodopi, 1990).

Bhabha, Homi (ed.), *Nation and Narration* (London: Routledge, 1990).

⸺ *The Location of Culture* (London: Routledge, 1994).

Boehmer, Elleke, *Colonial and Postcolonial Literature: Migrant Metaphors* (Oxford: Oxford University Press, 1995).

Bradbury, Malcolm, *The Modern British Novel* (Harmondsworth: Penguin, 1993).

Brooke-Rose, Christine, *Stories, Theories, and Things* (Cambridge: Cambridge University Press, 1991).

Chambers, Iain, and Curti, Linda (eds.), *The Post-Colonial Question* (London: Routledge, 1996).

Connor, Steven, *The English Novel in History: 1950–95* (London: Macmillan, 1996).

Cornwell, Neil, *The Literary Fantastic: From Gothic to Postmodernism* (New York: Harvester, 1990).

Cronin, Richard, *Imagining India* (London: Macmillan, 1989).

Dhawan, R. J. (ed.), *Three Contemporary Novelists: Khrishwant Singh, Chaman Nahal, Salman Rushdie* (New Delhi: Classical, 1985).

Doherty, Thomas (ed.), *Postmodernism: A Reader* (New York: Harvester, 1993).

Gasiorek, Andrzej, *Post-War British Fiction: Realism and After* (London: Arnold, 1995).

Gorra, Michael, *After Empire: Scott, Naipaul, Rushdie* (Chicago: Chicago University Press, 1997).

Hanne, Michael, *The Power of the Story: Fiction and Political Change* (Providence: Beghahn, 1994).

Jackson, Rosemary, *Fantasy: The Literature of Subversion* (London: Methuen, 1981).

King, Bruce, (ed.), *The Commonwealth Novel since 1960* (Houndmills: Macmillan, 1991).

Kirpal, Viney, *The Third World Novel of Expatriation* (New Delhi: Sterling, 1989).

—— *The New Indian Novel in English* (New Delhi: Allied, 1990).

Kundera, Milan, *Testaments Betrayed* (London: Faber, 1995).

Lee, Alison, *Realism and Power: Postmodern British Fiction* (London: Routledge, 1990).

Massie, Alan, *The Novel Today* (London: Longman, 1990).

McHale, Brian, *Postmodernist Fiction* (London: Methuen, 1987).

—— *Constructing Postmodernism* (London: Routledge, 1992).

Moore-Gilbert, Bart (ed.), *Writing India 1757–90: The Literature of British India* (Manchester: Manchester University Press, 1996).

Onega, Susana (ed.), *Telling Histories: Narrativizing History, Historicizing Literature* (Amsterdam: Rodopi, 1995).

Rai, Sudha, *Homeless by Choice: Naipaul, Jhabvala, Rushdie, and India* (Jaipur: Printwell, 1992).

Richetti, John (ed.), *The Columbia History of the British Novel* (New York: Columbia University Press, 1994).

Riemenschneider, Dieter (ed.), *Critical Approaches to the New Literatures in English* (Essen: Blaue Eule, 1989).

Scanlan, Margaret, *Traces of Another Time: History and Politics in Postwar British Fiction* (Princeton, NJ: Princeton University Press, 1990).

Sharma, Govind Narain (ed.), *Literature and Commitment* (Toronto: TSAR with the Canadian Association of Commonwealth Literature, 1988).

Simpson, Peter (ed.), *The Given Condition: Essays in Post-Colonial Literature* (Christchurch, NZ: 1995).

Singh, R. K. (ed.), *Indian English Writing: 1981–5* (New Delhi, Bahri, 1987).

Singh, Sushila (ed.), *Feminism and Recent Fiction in English* (New Delhi: Prestige, 1991).

Smyth, Edward (ed.), *Postmodernism and Contemporary Fiction* (London: Batsford, 1991).

Spivak, Gayatri Chakravorty, *Outside in the Teaching Machine* (London: Routledge, 1993).

Suleri, Sara, *The Rhetoric of English India* (Chicago: Chicago University Press, 1992).

Taylor, D. J., *After the War: Novel and English Society since 1945* (London: Chatto & Windus, 1993).

Tiffin, Chris, and Lawson, Alan (eds.), *De-Scribing Empire: Postcolonialism and Textuality* (London: Routledge, 1994).

Walsh, William, *Indian Literature in English* (London: Longman, 1990).

Waugh, Patricia, *Metafiction: The Theory and Practice of Self-Conscious Fiction* (London: Methuen, 1984).

—— *Practising Postmodernism* (London: Edward Arnold, 1992).

Wheale, Nigel (ed.), *Postmodern Arts* (London: Routledge, 1995).

White, Hayden, *The Content of the Form: Narrative Discourse and Historical Representation* (Baltimore: Johns Hopkins University Press, 1987).

Williams, Patrick, and Chrisman, Laura, *Colonial Discourse and Post-colonial Theory* (Hemel Hempstead: Harvester, 1993).

Young, Robert, *Colonial Desire: Hybridity in Theory, Culture, and Race* (London: Routledge, 1995).

Zamora, Lois Parkinson, and Faris, Wendy B. (eds.), *Magical Realism: Theory, History, Community* (Durham, NC: Duke University Press, 1995).

Articles

This selection lists only a small number of articles on Rushdie; mainly, those referred to in the present study. See Fletcher (ed.), *Reading Rushdie* (pp. 361–96), for an Annotated Bibliography of some 200 English-language articles, divided into sections on the different novels. Joel Kuortti's *Salman Rushdie Bibliography* lists over 2,000 articles of different kinds, more than half of which refer to the Rushdie Affair: see below. Articles on Rushdie appear in a wide variety of journals, those focusing on law, religion, politics, and race as well as those concerned with literature, history, and cultural studies.

Al-Azm, Sadik, 'The Importance of Being Earnest about Salman Rushdie', in Fletcher (ed.), *Reading Rushdie*, 255–92.

Aravamudan, Srinivas, 'The Novels of Salman Rushdie: Mediated Reality as Fantasy', *World Literature Today*, 63/1 (1989), 42–5.

────── '"Being God's Postman is no Fun, Yaar"', in Fletcher (ed.), *Reading Rushdie*, 187–208.

Bader, Rudolf, '*The Satanic Verses*: An Intercultural Experiment by Salman Rushdie', *International Fiction Review*, 19 (1992), 65–75.

Balasubramanian, Radha, 'The Similarities between Mikhail Bulgakov's *The Master and Margareta* and Salman Rushdie's *The Satanic Verses*', *International Fiction Review*, 22 (1995), 37–46.

Bardolph, Jacqueline, 'Language is Courage', in Fletcher (ed.), *Reading Rushdie*, 209–20.

Batty, Nancy E., 'The Art of Suspense: Rushdie's 1001 (Mid-)Nights', in Fletcher (ed.), *Reading Rushdie*, 69–82.

Bharucha, Rustom, 'Rushdie's Whale', in Fletcher (ed.), *Reading Rushdie*, 159–72.

Booker, M. Keith, 'Beauty and the Beast: Dualism as Despotism in the Fiction of Salman Rushdie', in Fletcher (ed.), *Reading Rushdie*, 237–54.

Brennan, Timothy, '*Shame*'s Holy Book, in Fletcher (ed.), *Reading Rushdie*, 109–22.

Brigg, Peter, 'Salman Rushdie's Novels: The Disorder in Fantastic Order', in Fletcher (ed.), *Reading Rushdie*, 173–86.

Cook, Rufus, 'Place and Displacement in Salman Rushdie's Work',

World Literature Today, 68/1 (1994), 23–8.

Cronin, Richard, 'The Indian English Novel: *Kim* and *Midnight's Children'*, *Modern Fiction Studies*, 33/2 (1987), 201–13.

Cundy, Catherine, ' "Rehearsing Voices": Salman Rushdie's *Grimus'*, in Fletcher (ed.), *Reading Rushdie*, 45–54.

Engblom, Philip, 'A Multitude of Voices: Carnivalization and Dialogicality in the Novels of Salman Rushdie', in Fletcher (ed.), *Reading Rushdie*, 295–305.

Fischer, Michael M., and Abedi, Mehdi, 'Bombay Talkies, the Word and the World: Salman Rushdie's *Satanic Verses'*, *Cultural Anthropology*, 5/2 (1990), 107–59.

Fletcher, M. D., 'Rushdie's *Shame* as Apologue', in Fletcher (ed.), *Reading Rushdie*, 97–108.

François, Pierre, 'Salman Rushdie's Philosophical Materialism in *The Satanic Verses'*, in Fletcher (ed.), *Reading Rushdie*, 305–20.

Grewal, Inderpal, 'Salman Rushdie: Marginality, Women, and *Shame'*, in Fletcher (ed.), *Reading Rushdie*, 123–44.

Hawes, Clement, 'Leading History by the Nose: The Turn to the Eighteenth Century in *Midnight's Children'*, *Modern Fiction Studies*, 39/1 (1993), 147–68.

Johansen, Ib, 'The Flight from the Enchanter: Reflections on Salman Rushdie's *Grimus'*, in Fletcher (ed.), *Reading Rushdie*, 23–34.

Jones, Peter, '*The Satanic Verses* and the Politics of Identity', in Fletcher (ed.), *Reading Rushdie*, 321–34.

Jussawalla, Feroza, 'Resurrecting the Prophet: the Case of Salman, the Otherwise', *Public Culture*, 2/1 (1989), 106–17.

—— 'Rushdie's *Dastan-e-Dilruba*: The Satanic Verses as Rushdie's Love Letter to Islam', *Diacritics*, 26 (1996), 50–73.

Kane, Jean, M., 'The Migrant Intellectual and the Body of History: Salman Rushdie's *Midnight's Children'*, *Contemporary Literature*, 37/1 (1996), 94–118.

Merivale, Patricia, 'Saleem Fathered by Oscar: Intertextual Strategies in *Midnight's Children* and *The Tin Drum'*, in Fletcher (ed.), *Reading Rushdie*, 83–96.

Needham, Anuradha Dingwaney, 'The Politics of Post-Colonial Identity in Salman Rushdie', in Fletcher (ed.), *Reading Rushdie*, 145–58.

Newell, Stephanie, 'The Other God: Salman Rushdie's "New" Aesthetic', *Literature in History*, 3rd ser., 1/2 (1992), 67–87.

Parameswaran, Uma, 'New Dimensions Courtesy of the Whirling Demons: Word-Play in *Grimus'*, in Fletcher (ed.), *Reading Rushdie*, 35–44.

Price, David, 'Salman Rushdie's "Use and Abuse of History" in *Midnight's Children'*, *Ariel*, 25/2 (1994).

Rhombes, N., Jr., '*The Satanic Verses* as Cinematic Narrative', *Literature/*

Film Quarterly, 11/1 (1993), 47–53.

Spivak, Gayatri, 'Reading *The Satanic Verses*', *Public Culture*, 2/1 (1989), 79–99.

Suleri, Sara, 'Contraband Histories: Salman Rushdie and the Embodiment of Blasphemy', in Fletcher (ed.), *Reading Rushdie*, 221–36.

Syed, Mujeebuddin, 'Warped Mythologies in Salman Rushdie's *Grimus*', *Ariel*, 25/4 (1994), 135–52.

_____ '*Midnight's Children* and its Indian Con-Texts', *Journal of Commonwealth Literature*, 29/2 (1994), 95–108.

Wilson, Keith, '*Midnight's Children* and Reader Responsibility', in Fletcher (ed.), *Reading Rushdie*, 55–68.

THE RUSHDIE AFFAIR

Collections of essays, letters, and documents

Appignanesi, Lisa, and Maitland, Sara (eds.), *The Rushdie File* (London: ICA/ Fourth Estate, 1989).

Cohn-Sherbok, Dan (ed.), *The Salman Rushdie Controversy in Inter-Religious Perspective* (Lewiston, NY, and Lampeter: Edward Mellen, 1990).

For Rushdie: Essays by Arab and Muslim Writers in Defense of Free Speech [no editor(s) identified] (New York: George Braziller, 1994). First published as *Pour Rushdie: Cent intellectuels arabes et musulmans pour la liberté d'expression* (Paris: Éditions la Découverte, 1993).

Horton, John (ed.), *Liberalism, Multiculturalism and Toleration* (London: Macmillan, 1993).

MacDonogh, Steven (ed.), in association with Article 19, *The Rushdie Letters: Freedom to Speak, Freedom to Write* (Dingle, Co. Derry: Brandon, 1993). This book includes a section 'Fiction, Fact, and the *Fatwa*' (pp. 125–83), an ongoing chronicle of events since the *fatwa* maintained by Carmel Bedford on behalf of the International Committee for the Defence of Salman Rushdie and his Publishers.

Three reports relating to the issue have been published by the Commission for Racial Equality and the Inter-Faith Network of the United Kingdom. These are: *Law, Blasphemy and the Multi-Faith Society: Seminar Report*, ed. Simon Lee *et al.* (1990); *Free Speech: Seminar Report*, ed. Susan Mendus *et al.* (1990); *Britain: A Plural Society*, ed. Sebastian Poulter *et al.* (1990).

The continuing series *Contemporary Literary Criticism* (Detroit: Gale) published two substantial entries on '*The Satanic Verses* Controversy' in volumes for 1989 (pp. 214–63), and 1990 (pp. 404–56).

Among journals to have dedicated special issues to the affair are:

American Atheist, 31/9 (1989).

Index on Censorship, 18/5 (May 89), and 19/4 (Apr. 90). *Index on Censorship* maintains a continuing watch on the affair in its regular feature 'Index Index', reviewing censorship issues and events worldwide.

Public Culture, 2/1 (Fall 1989).

Third Text, 11 (Summer 1990): 'Beyond the Rushdie Affair'.

See also: Tariq Modood, 'British Asian Muslims and the Rushdie Affair', *Political Quarterly*, 61/2 (Apr. 1990), 143–60.

Relevant monographs include:

Akhtar, Shabbir, *Be Careful With Muhammad! The Salman Rushdie Affair* (London: Bellew, 1989).

Easterman, Daniel, *New Jerusalems: Reflections on Islam, Fundamentalism, and the Rushdie Affair* (London: Grafton, 1992).

Kuortti, Joel, *Place of the Sacred: The Rhetoric of the* Satanic Verses *Affair* (Frankfurt: Peter Lang, 1997).

Lee, Simon, *The Cost of Free Speech* (London: Faber, 1990).

Pipes, Daniel, *The Rushdie Affair: The Novel, The Ayatollah, and the West* (New York: Carol/Birch Lane, 1990).

Ruthven, Malise, *A Satanic Affair: Salman Rushdie and the Rage of Islam* (London: Chatto, 1990; republished as *A Satanic Affair: Salman Rushdie and the Wrath of Islam*, 1991).

Sardar, Ziauddin, and Davies, Meryl Wyn, *Distorted Imagination: Lessons from the Rushdie Affair* (London: Grey Seal, 1990).

Weatherby, William, J., *Salman Rushdie: Sentenced to Death* (New York: Carroll & Graf, 1990).

Webster, Richard, *A Brief History of Blasphemy: Liberalism, Censorship, and 'The Satanic Verses'* (Southwold: Orwell, 1990).

See also the relevant sections in books by Alexander, Connor, Cornwell, Goonetilleke, Kundera, Spivak, and Wheale, listed above.

146

Index

Printed in the United Kingdom
by Lightning Source UK Ltd.
123874UK00001B/166-399/A